Oracle Performance Troubleshooting

With Dictionary Internals SQL & Tuning Scripts,
Second Edition

Robin Schumacher
Donald K. Burleson

This book is dedicated to the most important people in my life. To Jesus Christ for my eternal salvation, to my wonderful wife Laura who is more than I could ever ask for and certainly more than I deserve and to the two most precious little girls on the planet – Hannah and Claire – for being daddy's sweethearts and for causing a permanent smile to forever be affixed to my face.

Robin Schumacher

Oracle Performance Troubleshooting
With Dictionary Internals SQL & Tuning Scripts,
Second Edition

By Robin Schumacher and Donald K. Burleson

Published in Kittrell, North Carolina, USA.
Oracle In-Focus Series: Book # 36
Series Editor: Donald K. Burleson
Production Manager: Robin Rademacher
Production Editor: Valerre Aquitaine, Janet Burleson
Cover Design: Janet Burleson
Printing History: May 2003 First Edition, May 2010/March 2014 Second Edition

Oracle, Oracle7, Oracle8, Oracle8i, Oracle9i, Oracle10g and Oracle 11g are trademarks of Oracle Corporation.

Many of the designations used by computer vendors to distinguish their products are claimed as Trademarks. All names known by Rampant TechPress to be trademark names appear in this text as initial caps.

The information provided by the authors of this work is believed to be accurate and reliable. However, because of the possibility of human error by authors and editors, Rampant TechPress cannot guarantee the accuracy or completeness of any information included in this work and is not responsible for any errors, omissions, or inaccurate results obtained from the use of information, scripts, illustrations or code in this work.

ISBN 10: 0-9823061-7-2
ISBN 13: 978-0-9823061-7-8
Library of Congress Control Number: 2010905834

Table of Contents

Using the Online Code Depot

Purchase of this book provides complete access to the online code depot that contains sample code scripts. Any code depot scripts in this book are located at the following URL in zip format ready to load and use:

rampant.cc/oracle_troubleshooting2.htm

If technical assistance is needed with downloading or accessing the scripts, please contact Rampant TechPress at rtp@rampant.cc.

Conventions Used in this Book

It is critical for any technical publication to follow rigorous standards and employ consistent punctuation conventions to make the text easy to read. However, this is not an easy task. Within database terminology, there are many types of notation that can confuse a reader. For example, some Oracle utilities such as STATSPACK and TKPROF are always spelled in CAPITAL letters, while Oracle parameters and procedures have varying naming conventions in the database documentation. It is also important to remember that many database commands are case sensitive, and are always left in their original executable form, and never altered with italics or capitalization. Hence, all Rampant TechPress books follow these conventions:

Parameters: Database parameters will be *lowercase italics*. The exception is parameter arguments that are commonly capitalized (KEEP pool, TKPROF), which will be ALL CAPS.

Variables: Procedural language (e.g. PL/SQL) program variables and arguments will also remain in *lowercase italics* (i.e. *dbms_job*).

Tables & dictionary objects: Data dictionary objects are referenced in lowercase italics (*dba_indexes*, *v$sql*), including *v$* and *x$* views (*x$kcbcbh*, *v$parameter*) and dictionary views (*dba_tables*, *user_indexes*).

SQL: All SQL is formatted for easy use in the code depot and displayed in lowercase. Main SQL terms (select, from, where, group by, order by, having) will appear on a separate line.

Programs & Products: All products and programs that are known to the author are capitalized according to the vendor specifications (CentOS, VMware, Oracle, etc). All names known by Rampant TechPress to be trademark names appear in this text as initial caps. References to UNIX are always made in uppercase.

Acknowledgements

This type of highly technical reference book requires the dedicated efforts of many people. Even though we are the authors, our work ends when we deliver the content. After each chapter is delivered, several Oracle DBAs carefully review and correct the technical content. After the technical review, experienced copy editors polish the grammar and syntax.

The finished work is then reviewed as page proofs and turned over to the production manager, who arranges the creation of the online code depot and manages the cover art, printing distribution, and warehousing.

In short, the authors played a small role in the development of this book, and we need to thank and acknowledge everyone who helped bring this book to fruition:

Robin Rademacher for production management including the coordination of the cover art, page proofing, printing, and distribution.

Valerre Aquitaine for help in the production of the page proofs.

Janet Burleson for exceptional cover design, graphics and editing.

John Lavender for assistance with the web site and for creating the code depot and the online shopping cart for this book.

With sincerest thanks,

Robin Schumacher

Donald K. Burleson

Introduction to Oracle Troubleshooting

A good DBA is also a good detective

Introduction to Troubleshooting

One of the most stressful aspects of the Oracle DBA job role is troubleshooting acute performance problems. In a serious emergency, there could be thousands of end-users waiting for the DBA to provide access to the database. While the proactive techniques described in this book serve to prevent future performance problems, there is always the possibility of a rare exception, a rogue process, or an unplanned increase in system usage.

Hence, this book will focus on the "now" issues of Oracle emergency support and offer techniques to quickly locate and relieve transient Oracle bottlenecks.

It is also important to understand the scope of unplanned outages. The DBA may be troubleshooting a locked session for a single end-user, or could be troubleshooting a system-wide outage that affects thousands of end-users. This book will describe proven techniques and provide scripts to allow ease in ascertaining the cause of an acute performance problem, but problem identification is only a small part of the solution.

Even with all of Oracle's flexibility, some performance problems cannot be quickly corrected. These global lockups are often related to resource shortages that impact the entire database, and the solutions to these problems are often mandated by management.

While the DBA has a vested interest in finding the root cause of a performance problem, it is impractical to inconvenience an entire end-user community while performing diagnostics. Some mission-critical Oracle databases such as Amazon or eBay have downtime costs exceeding $100,000 per minute and time is of the essence when disaster strikes.

 **Do not be scared to bounce!**

If a production database has crashed, quickly abort and warm start. Bouncing a locked up instance will frequently fix the issue.

Oracle troubleshooting is part-and-parcel of Oracle tuning, an approach whereby the Oracle professional quickly diagnoses the root cause of an acute performance problem.

Huge stress levels and late night hours are an inevitable part of life for an emergency support DBA. Often the databases will be unfamiliar and there will only be a few minutes to view the problem and create a plan to quickly relieve the bottleneck. Only when the easy remedies have failed is the emergency support DBA called in because when a production database is in crisis, minimizing downtime is critical. At this point, clients demand quick fixes, and this often requires unconventional methods.

There are many global remedies, or silver bullets, for Oracle performance troubleshooting. Silver bullets are defined as any single action or small set of commands that quickly relieves an acute performance problem.

Some of these just-in-time tuning techniques have been codified in the Automatic Memory Management (AMM) facility, where the System Global Area (SGA) regions are morphed dynamically to meet changing demands of processing while others require manual intervention by the DBA.

Emergency Troubleshooting Methods

When the telephone rings at the database support desk, there is usually an irate end-user on the line complaining that their database is down. From this point forward, time is of the essence, and fast detective work must be done to get the database online again quickly. Functioning as an emergency Oracle support DBA can be great fun for any adrenaline junky. As illustrated in the following case studies, emergency Oracle support often requires a very different set of goals and techniques:

- **Fix the symptom first:** The goal is to make the database available as soon as possible, and it may be necessary to deliberately ignore the root cause and fix the symptom. The root cause can be addressed later, after the database is available to the end-user community.

- **Time is critical:** When a quick fix is required, instance-wide adjustments are often the best hope.

- **Be creative:** Traditional time consuming tuning methods do not always apply in an emergency.

Burleson Consulting provides an Oracle emergency support center (www.remote-dba.net) where calls are received from clients all over the world, each experiencing a serious loss of performance on their mission-critical Oracle databases. The authors have worked on systems where an Oracle failure has shut down entire factories, leaving thousands of workers sitting on their hands waiting for someone to do something to restart their assembly line. One of the authors, Don Burleson, has worked with hospital image delivery systems when patients were literally in surgery with their doctors waiting for the information they needed to save lives. He has also supported financial systems for which downtime is measured in tens of thousands of dollars per minute.

Working late nights as an emergency support DBA comes with huge stress levels, as previously stated. It is common to get calls from brand new clients and have only a few minutes to assess their crisis and devise a plan to quickly relieve the problem. This is the core of Oracle troubleshooting, hours of boredom punctuated by sheer terror.

Why Oracle Shops Lose Databases

For many shops, Oracle troubleshooting support is a last resort, and the DBAs call support only after the obvious remedies have already been tried.

While it is true that Oracle is unbreakable, it takes an experienced Oracle DBA to make sure that a mission-critical database never crashes.

It is not uncommon to get calls from shops that have no DBA or an inexperienced or inept DBA who cannot figure out the predicament! Here are some common reasons reported for having little or no on-site support:

- **Outsourced DBA:** Penny wise and pound foolish, shops fire their in-house DBA and buy cheap offshore support, and then call us after their database is hopelessly corrupted.

- **No DBA:** Having a good DBA can create the illusion that the company does not need a DBA because they never experience a database crash. This often slows the efforts to hire a replacement. For instance, it is frequently reported that the previous DBA quit six

---
\text{}

months ago, and there has not been time to find a replacement. Of course, this call follows the inevitable crash of the production instance.

- **Oracle Certified Beginners:** In many cases, the company has hired an Oracle ACE or an Oracle OCP, but despite their certificates, they do not know what they are doing. This is usually caused by their lack of any significant experience with real database systems.

The main theme of this book is "there are no rules in Oracle troubleshooting". It is the most exciting and challenging area of Oracle performance tuning. All rigorous methodologies are thrown by the wayside and the DBA should do whatever it takes to get the database back online as soon as possible.

Oracle Silver Bullet

For those who are old enough to remember the golden age of television, the term "silver bullet" refers to the Lone Ranger, who always carried a silver bullet, a magic weapon against evil, which has been believed in legends since the 1700s.

Of course, there is no magic in Oracle tuning, but there are techniques that can change the behavior of an entire database, both good and bad! Throughout this book, the term silver bullet will be used to describe any small DBA action that has a dramatic effect on the performance of a large portion of an Oracle database.

There are many silver bullets for Oracle performance tuning. A silver bullet simply contains a small set of commands that quickly relieves, or accentuates, an acute performance bottleneck. Some of these just-in-time tuning techniques have been codified in Oracle 10g via the AMM, in which the SGA regions are changed dynamically to meet the changing demands of the application.

While there is no substitute for good database design, well-coded PL/SQL and optimized SQL, the Oracle DBA often has no control over the quality of these components. Silver bullets are sometimes the only solutions that remain for the Oracle DBA for any number of reasons.

Tight-Fisted Management

Management will commonly be unwilling to pay to solve the root cause of an Oracle performance problem. Managers are driven by cost savings and they are extremely averse to taking risks.

For example, instead of paying $100,000 to tune 1,000 SQL statements, the manager may instead spend $50,000 to move poor SQL to a faster server.

Embarrassed Management

Management may not want to publicly acknowledge that their bargain Oracle application was poorly designed. Even if the DBA proves that the Oracle schema needs a total reconstruction, the manager may not be willing to expose their poor judgment.

Embarrassed Vendors

Most vendor packages are designed with extremely generic SQL so that they can be easily ported to a variety of database platforms such as SQL Server, MySQL, and DB2, and they rarely make customization for Oracle-centric performance. Worst of all, most vendors do not like being told that their Oracle database layer needs to be tuned.

Vendors control the schema structures and the application layers. Even if a user finds suboptimal SQL statements, they often cannot access the SQL source code in order to tune it.

These quirky vendor packages are the primary reason that Oracle offers specialized features such as optimizer plan stability in the form of stored outlines and the new Oracle 10g SQL Profiles feature. In fact, Oracle has a wealth of tools for tuning vendor applications when the source code cannot be altered.

The Limitations of the DBA

There are many database problem areas that are beyond the scope of the Oracle DBA's control, and this can be very frustrating. The following is a short list of Oracle problems that the DBA may be prohibited from fixing:

- Poorly designed application or schema
- Inefficient PL/SQL within the application
- Excessive Transparent Network Substrate (TNS) calls within the application
- Dynamic SQL
- SQL without host variables
- Poorly-formed SQL statements
- Suboptimal server kernel parameters

So, do these bindings mean that the Oracle DBA is powerless to tune the database? No, of course it does not. The DBA has a wealth of tuning tools at their disposal and many of these tools can have a positive effect on an entire database. The silver bullet approach allows for the tuning of many performance issues when the code cannot be changed directly.

To see how Oracle troubleshooting works in the real world, examine some case studies in Oracle emergency techniques.

Case Studies in Oracle Troubleshooting

Unlike traditional tuning where the performance changes are justified with empirical benchmark tests, an emergency Oracle DBA has no such luxury. Emergency DBAs must use every weapon at their disposal to get the client running as quickly as possible. These unconventional methods are almost always driven by the client who does not appreciate the benefits of an elegant, long-term fix for the root cause of the problem. Clients are impatient, and they often insist on symptom-treating, stop-gap remedies that are neither elegant nor comprehensive. In many cases, the client does not want to hear about the time-consuming tasks that are required to address the root cause of the problem.

Contrary to the pontifications of theoreticians and ivory-tower academics, there are many silver bullets for Oracle performance tuning. Silver bullet in this instance means a small set of commands that quickly relieves an acute performance bottleneck. Take a close look at the real world silver bullets that one of the authors has encountered over many years of doing emergency Oracle support. The following stories are true, verifiable accounts of Oracle databases in which a fast fix was used to relieve an acute performance problem:

- Fix missing CBO statistics (or set *optimizer_mode=rule*)
- Replace an obsolete statistics gathering method
- Initialize missing Oracle instance parameters
- Add missing indexes
- Implement *cursor_sharing=force*

- Implement the KEEP pool for small-table full-scanned tables
- Change the CBO optimizer parameters
- Add additional SGA RAM
- Employ materialized views
- Create bitmap indexes
- Add freelists
- Windows Oracle issues

To those scientist DBAs who demand proof that these methods worked, they will not be found in this book. Most of the production systems that have been tuned have hundreds of segments and thousands of concurrent users. Trying to test a hypothesis on a large running database is like trying to tune a car while it is flying down the freeway at 75 miles per hour.

It is impossible to reproduce the conditions of a complex performance breakdown, and the emergency support DBA is forced to rely on experience and anecdotal evidence to guide their actions. Examine each of these silver bullets and see how a well-placed silver bullet can save the day.

Case Study: Troubleshoot Missing CBO Statistics

The call came in from an Oracle 9i client who had just moved their system into production and was experiencing a serious performance problem. Upon inspection, *optimizer_mode*=choose was found and only one table had been analyzed with statistics. The DBA said that she was running cost-based and she seemed totally unaware of the requirement to analyze the schema for CBO statistics. Here is how I recall the conversation:

DB: *"How are you collecting statistics?"*

DBA: *"We have BMC Patrol."*

DB: "No, No, how are you getting your SQL optimizer statistics?"

DBA: "The Oracle sales rep said that the CBO was intelligent, so I assumed it was getting its own statistics."

In a way, she was right. The problem started when she wanted to know the average row length for a table. She did a Google search and discovered that it was in the *dba_tables.avg_row_len* column. When she found it null, she went to MetaLink and learned that a *dbms_stats* command would fill in the *avg_row_len* column.

⟫ Code Depot Username = reader, Password = troubleshoot

As is known, when using *optimizer_mode=choose* with only one table analyzed, any SQL that touches the table will be optimized as a cost-based query, and the CBO will dynamically estimate statistics for all tables with missing statistics. In this case, a multi-step silver bullet did the trick:

```
alter table customer delete statistics;
exec dbms_stats (…);
```

The system immediately returned to an acceptable performance level, and the DBA learned about the importance of providing complete and timely statistics for the CBO using the *dbms_stats* utility. This case study highlights one reason why Oracle 10g was modified to automatically collect complete CBO statistics.

Case Study: Troubleshoot Obsolete CBO Statistics Gathering

In this emergency, a shop called complaining about a serious degradation in SQL performance right after implementing partitioned tablespaces in a 16-CPU Solaris 64-bit Oracle 9.0.4 system. They said that they thoroughly tested the change in their development and QA instances, and they could not understand why their system was grinding to a halt.

Upon inspection, it turned out that they were using *analyze table* and *analyze index* commands to gather their CBO statistics. Only the *dbms_stats* utility gathers partition-wise statistics. There was not time to pull a deep-sample collection, so a *dbms_stats* was issued with a 10 percent sample size. Note that I parallelized it with 15 parallel processes to speed up the statistics collection:

```
exec dbms_stats.gather_schema_stats( -
   ownname          => 'SAPR4', -
   options          => 'GATHER AUTO', -
   estimate_percent => 10, -
   method_opt       => 'for all columns size repeat', -
   degree           => 15 -
)
```

This took less than 30 minutes and the improved CBO statistics tripled the performance of the entire database.

Case Study: Troubleshoot Missing Oracle Instance Parameters

A call was received from a client in California who said that their performance was getting progressively worse as more customers accessed the Oracle database. Upon inspection, I discovered that their *db_cache_size* parameter was not present in the *init.ora* file. A quick instance bounce to reset *sga_max_size* and *db_cache_size* resulted in a 400 percent performance improvement.

In another memorable case, I received a call from a data warehouse client in California who complained that their performance degraded as the database grew. A quick look revealed that the *sort_area_size* parameter was missing and defaulting to a tiny value. Again, a change of *sort_area_size*=1048575, a quick bounce of the instance, and overall database performance improved by more than 50 percent.

Case Study: Troubleshoot Missing Indexes

An Oracle financial application shop in New York called and said that their performance degraded as more data was entered into the tables. A quick check of *v$sql_plan* using my *plan9i.sql* script looked like this:

```
                        Full table scans and counts

OWNER       NAME                       NUM_ROWS  C  K   BLOCKS   NBR_FTS
----------  ------------------------   --------  -  -  --------  -------
APPLSYS     FND_CONC_RELEASE_DISJS        14,293 N            4,293  498,864
APPLSYS     FND_CONC_RELEASE_PERIODS     384,173 N           67,915  134,864
DONALD      PERSON_LOGON_ID           18,263,390 N          634,272   96,212
DONALD      SITE_AMDMNT                2,371,232 N           51,020   50,719
DONALD      CLIN_PTCL_VIS_MAP         23,123,384 N          986,395   11,273
```

This shows a huge number of large-table, full-table scans. A quick look into *v$sql* revealed that the rows returned by each query was small, and a common WHERE clause for many queries looked like this:

```
WHERE customer_status = ':v1' and customer_age > :v2;
```

A quick creation of a concatenated index on *customer_status* and *customer_age* resulted in a 50x performance improvement and reduced disk I/O by over 600 percent.

In another memorable case on an 8.1.6 database, my *access.sql* script revealed suspect large-table, full-table scans:

```
                       Full table scans and counts

OWNER       NAME                       NUM_ROWS   C K   BLOCKS   NBR_FTS
----------  --------------------       -----------  - -  --------  -------
APPLSYS     FND_CONC_RELEASE_DISJS      1,293,292  N K  65,282    498,864
APPLSYS     FND_CONC_RELEASE_PERIODS    4,373,362  N K  62,282    122,764
APPLSYS     FND_CONC_RELEASE_STATES       974.193  N K   9,204     98,122
APPLSYS     FND_CONC_PP_ACTIONS           715,021  N      6,309     52,036
APPLSYS     FND_CONC_REL_CONJ_MEMBER       95,292  N K   4,409     23,122
```

The DBA had created an index on the *order_date* column and was surprised that their *order_date* index was not being used, primarily because their boss was not willing to pay for him to attend an Oracle 8 new features class. Creating the function-based index on *to_char(order_date, 'MON-DD')* resulted in an immediate 5x performance improvement.

Case Study: Troubleshoot CBO Optimizer Parameters

Another emergency situation involved an Oracle 9.0.2 client from Phoenix who called complaining about steadily degrading performance. A quick look into *v$sql_plan* view using my *plan9i.sql* script revealed loads of suspected unnecessary large-table, full-table scans.

Prior to Oracle 10g, adjusting optimizer parameters was the only way to compensate for shortcomings with *dbms_stats*. As of 10g, the use of *dbms_stats.gather_system_stats* and improved sampling within *dbms_stats* have made adjustments to these parameters far less important.

In this case, the top SQL was extracted from *v$sql* and timed as-is and with an *index* hint. The query with the *index* hint ran almost 20x faster, but it was unclear why the CBO was not choosing the index. This was a production emergency, and I did not have the luxury of investigating the root cause of the CBO issue.

I had to act fast, so I ran a script against *v$bh* and *user_indexes* and discovered that approximately 65 percent of the indexes were currently inside the data buffer cache. Based on similar systems, I decided to lower *optimizer_index_cost_adj* to a value of 20, hopefully forcing the CBO to lower the relative costs of index access.

```
optimizer_index_cost_adj=20
optimizer_index_caching=65
```

If the system in question is Oracle 9i and beyond, some parameters can be dynamically altered:

```
alter system set optimizer_index_cost_adj=20 scope = pfile;
```

This quick fix changed the execution plans for over 350 SQL statements and cut by half the overall system response time. The client was elated, and I was then able to take my time and investigate the root cause of the problem.

Ceteris Parabus, always adjust CBO statistics before adjusting optimizer parameters.

Case Study: Troubleshoot *cursor_sharing=force*

I worked on an Oracle database in Toronto where the end users complained about poor performance right after a new manufacturing plant was added to the existing database. A quick look at the STATSPACK top five timed events showed something like this:

```
Top 5 Wait Events
~~~~~~~~~~~~~~~~~                             Wait        % Total
Event                           Waits     Time (cs)     Wt Time
-------------------------- ------------  ------------  -------
enqueue                          25,901       479,654    46.71
db file scattered read       10,579,442       197,205    29.20
db file sequential read         724,325       196,583     9.14
latch free                    1,150,979        51,084     4.97
log file parallel write         148,932        39,822     3.88
```

My first look was into the SQL section of the STATSPACK report, where I noted that almost all of the SQL used "literals" in the WHERE clause of all queries.

```
WHERE customer_state = 'Alabama' and customer_type = 'REDNECK';
```

This was a vendor package with dynamically generated SQL, so *cursor_sharing* was the only fast solution. Setting *cursor_sharing=force* greatly reduced the contention on the library cache and reduced CPU consumption. In this emergency, the end users reported a 75 percent improvement in overall performance.

Case Study: Troubleshoot Small-table, Full-scanned Tables

I worked on a database recently in New Zealand that was running 9.2.0.4 and had a 16-CPU Solaris server with 8GB of RAM. The complaint was that performance had been degrading since the last production change. A STATSPACK top-five timed events report showed that over 80 percent of system waits related to db file scattered reads.

A quick review of *v$sql_plan* using *plan9i.sql* showed quite a few small-table, full-table scans with many of the tables not assigned to the KEEP pool, as denoted by the K column in the listing below:

```
                   Full table scans and counts


OWNER        NAME                    NUM_ROWS C K    BLOCKS  NBR_FTS
----------   ---------------------   -------- - -  --------  --------
APPLSYS      FND_CONC_RELEASE_DISJS        39 N          44    98,864
APPLSYS      FND_CONC_RELEASE_PERIODS      39 N K        21    78,232
APPLSYS      FND_CONC_RELEASE_STATES        1 N K         2    66,864
APPLSYS      FND_CONC_PP_ACTIONS        7,021 N       1,262    52,036
APPLSYS      FND_CONC_REL_CONJ_MEMBER       0 N K       322    50,174
APPLSYS      FND_FILE_TEMP                  0 N         544    48,611
APPLSYS      FND_RUN_REQUESTS              99 N          98    48,606
INV          MTL_PARAMETERS                 6 N K        16    21,478
APPLSYS      FND_PRODUCT_GROUPS             1 N          23    12,555
APPLSYS      FND_CONCURRENT_QUEUES_TL      13 N K        10    12,257
AP           AP_SYSTEM_PARAMETERS_ALL       1 N K         6     4,521
```

Rows fetched into the *db_cache_size* from full-table scans are not pinged to the Most-Recently-Used (MRU) end of the data buffer. Running my *buf_blocks.sql* script confirmed that the FTS blocks were falling off the Least-Recently-Used (LRU) end of the buffer, and had to be frequently reloaded into the buffer.

```
                       Contents of Data Buffers

              Number of Percentage
                                     Blocks in of object
               Object        Object  Buffer  Buffer Buffer   Block
Owner          Name          Type    Cache   Blocks Pool     Size
------------   -----------   -----   ------- ------ ------   ------
DW01           WORKORDER     TAB PART 94,856      6 DEFAULT   8,192
DW01           HOUSE         TAB PART 50,674      7 DEFAULT  16,384
ODSA           WORKORDER     TABLE    28,481      2 DEFAULT  16,384
DW01           SUBSCRIBER    TAB PART 23,237      3 DEFAULT   4,096
ODS            WORKORDER     TABLE    19,926      1 DEFAULT   8,192
DW01           WRKR_ACCT_IDX INDEX     8,525      5 DEFAULT  16,384
DW01           SUSC_SVCC_IDX INDEX     8,453     38 KEEP     32,768
```

In this case, I ran my *buf_keep_pool.sql* script to reassign all tables that experienced small-table, full-table scans into the KEEP pool. The output looks like this, and can be fed directly into SQL*Plus:

```
alter TABLE BOM.BOM_OPERATIONAL_ROUTINGS storage (buffer_pool keep);
alter INDEX BOM.CST_ITEM_COSTS_U1 storage (buffer_pool keep);
alter TABLE INV.MTL_ITEM_CATEGORIES storage (buffer_pool keep);
alter TABLE INV.MTL_ONHAND_QUANTITIES storage (buffer_pool keep);
alter TABLE INV.MTL_SUPPLY_DEMAND_TEMP storage (buffer_pool keep);
```

```
alter TABLE PO.PO_REQUISITION_LINES_ALL storage (buffer_pool keep);
alter TABLE AR.RA_CUSTOMER_TRX_ALL storage (buffer_pool keep);
alter TABLE AR.RA_CUSTOMER_TRX_LINES_ALL storage (buffer_pool keep);
```

With more efficient buffer caching, I fixed the problem in less than one hour and overall database performance more than doubled.

Case Study: Troubleshoot SGA RAM

One of the most common silver bullets is databases that have a working set of frequently referenced data that cannot fit into the data buffer cache. This used to be a huge problem for the 32-bit Oracle server in which the total SGA size was difficult to grow beyond 1.7GB without special tricks like AWE and NUMA. However, I still routinely see databases on dedicated servers with 8GB RAM with a SGA size less than 500MB. A quick increase in *db_block_buffers* or *db_cache_size* and performance improves dramatically.

Case Study: Tune with Materialized Views

Once there was a call from a point-of-sale data warehouse in Germany. The IT manager spoke very little English and most of the conversation was done using Babelfish. The system was largely read-only with a short batch window for nightly updates. Once I connected, I immediately noticed that virtually every query in the system was performing a *sum()* or *avg()* function against several key tables.

The *v$sql_plan* view, via *plan9i.sql,* showed loads of very large-table, full-table scans, and the system was crippled with db file scattered read waits.

```
Top 5 Timed Events
~~~~~~~~~~~~~~~~~~~~~                              % Total
Event                              Waits     Time (s)  Ela Time
----------------------------  ------------  ----------  --------
db file scattered read            325,519      3,246     82.04
library cache load lock             4,673      1,363      9.26
db file sequential read           534,598      7,146      4.54
CPU time                            1,154        645      3.83
log file parallel write            19,157        837      1.68
```

Figure 1.1: *Example of db File Scattered Read Waits*

I was easily able to help by creating three materialized views and employing query rewrite to reduce physical disk I/O by over 2,000 percent; this improved performance by more than 30x — a real silver bullet!

Case Study: Implement Bitmap Indexes

I was called upon to troubleshoot and fix a State Police query system that was experiencing slow query performance. The system was read-only except for a 30-minute window at night for data loading. Upon inspection of the SQL, I noted complex combinational WHERE clauses:

```
WHERE color='BLU' and make='CHEVY' and year=1997 and doors=2;
```

The distinct values for each of these columns were less than 200, and concatenated indexes were employed. Replacing the b-tree indexes with bitmap indexes resulted in a stunning performance improvement for the entire system, taking queries from three seconds down to under one-tenth of a second.

Case Study: Adding Freelists

A client called from Michigan with a complaint that the company order-processing center was unable keep up with adding new orders into Oracle. The client had just expanded its telephone order-processing department and had doubled the order processing staff to meet a surge in market interest. The VP was frantic, saying that 400 order-entry clerks were getting 30-second response time and they were forced to manually write down order information.

I checked *v$session* and found 450 connected users, and a quick review of *v$sql* revealed that at virtually all the DML were inserts into a *customer_order* table. The top timed event was *buffer busy wait* and it was clear that there were enqueues on the segment header blocks for the table and its indexes.

The supposedly proper fix for this issue is to create a new tablespace for the table and index using Automatic Segment Space Management (ASSM), also known as bitmap freelists. I could then reorganize the table online with the *dbms_redefinition* utility and *alter index cust_pk rebuild* the index into the new tablespace. However, it would take me several hours to build and execute the jobs and the VP said that he was losing over $500 per minute.

The system was on release 9.2.0.4, so I was able to immediately relieve the segment header contention with these commands:

```
alter table customer_order freelists 5;
alter index cust_pk freelists 5;
```

Note: I did not know the length of the enqueues on the segment header, so I added the additional freelists, one at a time, until the buffer busy waits disappeared.

Adding the additional freelists did the trick and the segment header contention disappeared. However, I knew that this was only a stop-gap fix and as soon as they ran their weekly purge, a single process, that only one of the five freelists would get the released blocks, causing the table to extend unnecessarily.

Case Study: Troubleshoot Windows Issues

Windows Oracle databases are always the most fun to tune because they are often implemented by someone with a very limited knowledge of Oracle. The following are my favorite Windows Oracle silver bullets.

- Norton AntiVirus: I got a call from a new client in England who said that their database had slowed to the point where sub-second queries were taking 15 minutes. A review of a STATSPACK report showed giant waits of up to 10 seconds on read I/O. A review of the external Windows environment revealed that a well-intentioned support person was told to install Norton AntiVirus on all Windows servers. Upon every block read, Norton was conducting a virus check!

- A really cool screen saver: Another case involved a Windows Oracle system that was experiencing sporadic CPU shortages, periods when over half of the CPU was being consumed by some external process. Because I was dialed in, I could not see the obvious. An on-site person informed me that the screen saver was called 3D Flowerbox. This was a hugely CPU-intensive screen saver that performed thousands of calculations per second to generate the cool display.

There are about a dozen silver bullet parameters which have a profound impact on performance, both good and bad. Adjusting these powerful throttles such as *optimizer_index_cost_adj*, and *_optimizer_cost_model* should only be done by experts, and only after the CBO statistics have been optimized, especially intelligent histogram placement.

Summary

This chapter was an introduction to troubleshooting an Oracle database. Several case studies were given illustrating a few ways in which clients needed assistance in improving performance or repairing their database and how emergency support was provided.

Now move on and take a closer look at Oracle troubleshooting.

Oracle Troubleshooting Specifics

Measuring Oracle Performance

Every Oracle professional would like to be thought of as a performance-tuning expert. Slow systems are the bane of existence for any critical business, and DBAs and developers alike constantly strive to improve their diagnostic skills. The world's Oracle consultants who make the really big money are the ones who can take a lethargic system and quickly turn it into one that runs as fast as greased lightning.

With the Internet, there is a wealth of information about Oracle troubleshooting and some of it is good, while most of it is absolute garbage. Every self-anointed Oracle expert is touting their own methodology for Oracle troubleshooting, and some are absolute zealots in proclaiming their approach as the "best" method. In the real world, an Oracle troubleshooting expert uses a variety of tools and techniques and there is no single best way to diagnose an acute performance problem.

Oracle analysts use one of two methods for examining the performance levels of a database in crisis. Note that this is not about the holistic, proactive tuning approaches which are used for long-term tuning. This is about the reactive methods to see what the problem may be in real-time.

- Wait event analysis: Advocates of the Oracle wait interface (OWI and ASH) examine the instance to see where Oracle is spending the most time.

- Trace dump analysis: Some Oracle experts say that the only way to see what is going on is to collect a detailed trace dump (event 10046) and analyze where Oracle is spending its time.

- Ratio-based analysis: Some experts use short-term ratios to pinpoint areas of poor performance. Ever since the Oracle 7 performance tuning class in the early 1990s recommended keeping the buffer hit ratio above 95%, advice later adopted by SAP and other ERP vendors, there has been a huge amount of misunderstandings about the Buffer Cache Hit Ratio (BCHR), and the value of ratios in general as a tool for Oracle monitoring and tuning.

- Bottleneck analysis: This seems to be more in vogue today with many experts on database performance deriding those who still dare to practice any ratio-based analysis. Instead of using ratios, this methodology focuses on finding the things that cause the database to wait, and removing them where possible.

Start by separating the fact from the fiction. Whether it is about the BCHR or the data buffer cache advisory (see *v$db_cache_advice*), it is good to remember that they are just different formulas for twiddling the same metrics, namely the elapsed-time deltas for logical I/O (consistent gets) and physical I/O (disk reads). Hence, any computations are fundamentally flawed:

- One point: A single delta value does not provide enough information for any meaningful estimates.

- Too long: Using the standard one-hour snapshots loses much detail, making most extrapolations meaningless. Of course, it is a different story when multiple snapshots are being taken, especially at high-granularity, e.g. 10 minutes or less.

If the problem is decomposed, elapsed logical I/O vs. physical reads is the main concern. The formulas are incidental.

Most experts agree that the BCHRs by themselves are of limited value, only one of hundreds of metrics that indicate database performance. In general, all ratios are limited because they only measure a probability; in the instance case, the overall probability that a data block will be found in the data buffer cache upon re-read, i.e. the BCHR has no bearing on blocks that are brand new to the data cache.

Another issue with the BCHR is its high variability. For example, while an overall hourly BCHR may be 96%, the value swings wildly. When examined at a finer level of granularity, the BCHR could be 20% one minute, and 95% the next. It is all dependent on the current workload.

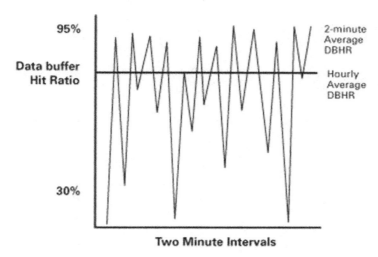

Figure 2.1: *High Variability of BCHR*

So, can it be concluded that the ratios are totally useless? This will be examined next.

The BCHR for Performance Tuning

The buffer cache hit ratio is no longer touted as a standalone measure of system performance, but it is not completely useless either. From the Oracle documentation on memory usage, it can be seen that Oracle continues to recommend using the BCHR in conjunction with other metrics, namely the predictive ratios displayed in the 10g buffer cache advisory:

"The buffer cache hit ratio can be used to verify the physical I/O as predicted by *v$db_cache_advice*."

In a well-tuned production database, adding RAM to the data buffers can make a difference in overall throughput via a reduction in physical disk reads, one of the most time-consuming operations in any Oracle database. The Oracle AWR report contains a buffer advisory utility that shows predictions of the marginal changes to physical disk reads with changes to the buffer size:

```
Buffer Pool Advisory
-> Only rows with estimated physical reads >0 are displayed
-> ordered by Block Size, Buffers For Estimate
  Size for Size Buffers for Est Physical Estimated
P Estimate (M) Factr Estimate Read      Factor    Physical Reads
--- ------------ ----- ---------- ------------- ------------------
D            4    .1        501         2.10         1,110,930
D            8    .2      1,002         1.84           970,631
D           12    .2      1,503         1.75           924,221
D           16    .3      2,004         1.62           857,294
D           20    .4      2,505         1.61           850,849
D           24    .5      3,006         1.59           837,223
D           28    .5      3,507         1.58           831,558
D           32    .6      4,008         1.57           829,083
D           36    .7      4,509         1.56           825,336
D           40    .8      5,010         1.56           823,195
D           44    .8      5,511         1.06           557,204
D           48    .9      6,012         1.01           534,992
D           52   1.0      6,513         1.00           527,967
D           56   1.1      7,014         0.78           411,218
D           60   1.2      7,515         0.35           186,842
D           64   1.2      8,016         0.28           148,305
D           68   1.3      8,517         0.26           134,969
D           72   1.4      9,018         0.23           123,283
D           76   1.5      9,519         0.23           121,878
D           80   1.5     10,020         0.23           120,317
-------------------------------------------------------------
```

For a well-tuned database, the goal of setting the data buffer size is to cache the working set of frequently referenced data blocks, the point at which there is a marginal decline in the amount of RAM needed to reduce disk reads (Figure 2.2).

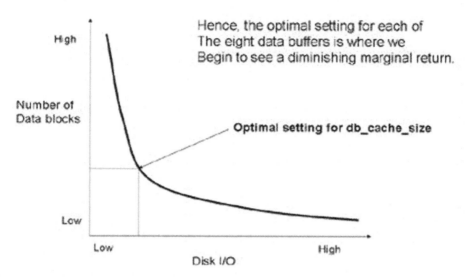

Figure 2.2: *Diminishing Marginal Returns and Buffer Utilization*

Oracle Enterprise Manager (OEM) also displays the data buffer advisor, and it has an interactive feature whereby the cache size can be changed in real-time (Figure 2.3).

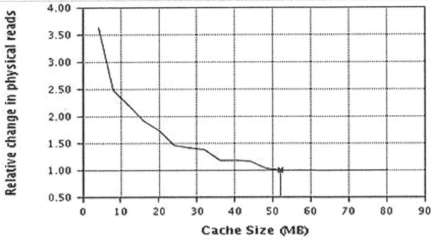

Buffer Cache Size Advice

Figure 2.3: *Data Buffer Advisor in OEM*

However, there are some serious limitations to the Oracle data buffer cache advisor:

- Only one delta: Using only two observations for logical reads and physical I/O are not enough data for a meaningful prediction. The current workload assumption has a wide variance, and the numbers for a one-minute report will be quite different from an one-hour report.

- Only two metrics: All of the advice from the data buffer cache advisory is limited to logical I/O and physical I/O at the system-wide level.

- Assumption of optimization: The AWR data buffer cache advisor, and possibly the related *v$db_cache_advice* utility, only has two data points to consider and it assumes that the existing data buffer size is optimal, the point at which the working set of frequently used data blocks are cached, and additions to the data buffer result in marginally declining reductions in physical reads.

Hence, on the margin, the data buffer cache advisory is inaccurate for a database with an undersized *db_cache_size* and *db_keep_cache_size* and such. With the data buffer set to a very small size, a small increase to the size of the RAM data buffers results in a large reduction in Disk I/O (Figure 2.4).

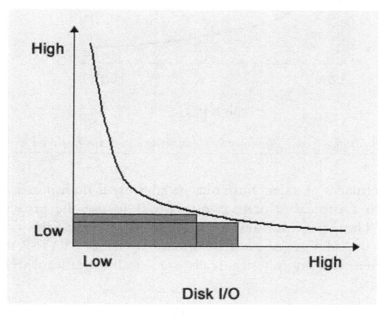

Figure 2.4: *The Buffer Advisory in Regards to Small Cache*

However, the high reduction in disk I/O does not continue ad infinitum. As the RAM size approaches the database size, the marginal reduction in disk I/O is smaller because all databases have infrequently accessed data, as shown in Figure 2.5.

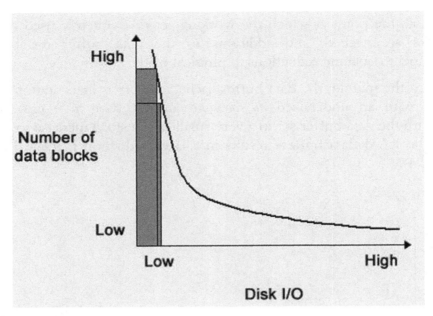

Figure 2.5: *Data Buffer Cache Advisory Not Knowing Cache is Oversized*

In sum, the usefulness of a data buffer cache advisory is undisputed, but the true way to a successful predictive model is to use the proactive tuning scripts. These provide valid time-series analyses since the single delta values in the advisory are not sufficient. By using STATSPACK data for consistent gets and physical reads, statistically significant trends can be established.

When done properly, ratio-based analysis definitely has a place in one's performance-tuning arsenal. Performance ratios are very good roll-up mechanisms for busy DBAs, making analysis possible at a glance. Many DBAs have large database farms to contend with and cannot spend time checking detailed wait-based analysis outputs for each and every database they oversee.

For example, take a look at one of the common queries used to report the database's BCHR:

```
select
   100 -
   100 *
   (round((sum (decode (name, 'physical reads', value, 0)) -
    sum (decode (name, 'physical reads direct', value, 0))) /
   (sum (decode (name, 'db block gets', value, 1)) +
    sum (decode (name, 'consistent gets', value, 0)))),3))
from
   sys.v_$sysstat
where
   name in ('db block gets', 'consistent gets',
            'physical reads', 'physical reads direct')
```

If a database has been up for many weeks, the numbers representing the I/O statistics above will likely be enormous. The counts of block gets and consistent gets will be very large and, in most systems, exceed the count of physical reads by a wide margin. Such a situation can skew the buffer cache hit ratio if it is computed solely with cumulative value counts in *v$sysstat*.

If an inefficient SQL query is issued that causes many physical reads, adding them to the *v$sysstat* counters will probably not cause a meaningful dip in the overall buffer cache hit ratio as long as cumulative statistics are used. However, if delta statistics are used - taking, for a specified sampling period, the before and after counts of each statistic that make up the ratio - then the portrayal of the buffer cache hit ratio will be more current and accurate.

There are some ratios that do not rely on *v$sysstat*, and therefore, can be derived from current/cumulative values. One example of this is the blocking lock ratio, which computes the percentage of user sessions that are currently blocked on a system. Because locks in a database are repeatedly obtained and released, the ratio can be computed with cumulative numbers from several performance views without the need for taking a before-and-after statistical snapshot.

In addition to using delta statistics to compute many of the key metrics in ratio-based performance analysis, the DBA must also be committed to examining all the database categories that contribute to its overall health and well-being. This can mean employing ratios and analytic percentages that have historically been neglected by DBAs.

For instance, many DBAs do not use ratios when examining their object structures in a database because they have not seen how such a technique can be applied to objects. However, ratio-based analysis can definitely be utilized to determine if objects like tables and indexes are disorganized. For example, finding the global percentage of tables that contain chained rows may help the DBA realize that he is not properly defining the table storage parameters in a dynamic database.

A final thing to remember about using ratio-based analysis is that while there are several rules of thumb that can be used as starting points in the evaluation of database performance, each database has an individual personality. Some hard and fast rules simply will not apply to every database.

The Danger of Relying on Blanket Ratios

The danger in using blanket ratio standards is that they can lead one to take action haphazardly, often contributing nothing to the situation and sometimes even degrading performance! For example, one rule of thumb says that the library cache hit ratio should never fall below 95%, and if it does, the standard remedy is to increase the amount of memory assigned to the shared pool.
But it is never that simple, and this kind of lazy approach to performance tuning can actually lead to more problems. Oftentimes, a database that is very ad-hoc in nature will experience many queries that are almost always unique with respect to their WHERE clause predicates and the literals used as qualifying filters.

So, does ratio-based analysis still sound like old hat or can it add value to one's performance analysis arsenal? Now that the benefits and shortcomings of ratio-based analysis are understood, it is time to continue into the next section and discover the ins-and-outs of Oracle bottleneck analysis.

Oracle Bottleneck Analysis

When an Oracle database is up and running, every connected process is either busy doing work or waiting to perform work. A process that is waiting may be idle, or it can be an indicator that a database bottleneck exists. How to tell the difference? This is where bottleneck analysis comes into play. This form of performance analysis can be used to determine if perceived bottlenecks in a database are contributing to a performance problem.

Bottleneck analysis is a valid method of measuring performance because it helps track where the database has been spending its time. If latch contention or heavy table-scan activity has been dragging a database's performance down, use bottleneck analysis to confirm the actual root cause. Once one or more wait events or other bottlenecks have been pinpointed as possible performance vampires, the DBA can drill down and oftentimes discover a fair amount of detail about the sessions and objects that are causing the problem.

Prerequisites for Bottleneck Analysis

How does one correctly practice bottleneck or wait-based analysis? First, it is imperative that the *timed_statistics* initialization parameter be set to TRUE if the Oracle wait events are to be examined. By default, this parameter is set to FALSE, which disallows the collection of wait times for each wait event defined in the Oracle engine.

To really understand the impact of wait events on database performance, needing to not only discover what the database is or has been waiting on but the durations of the waits is an important component. Having both allows a complete picture to be formed regarding the magnitude of wait-initiated performance degradations. Almost all Oracle experts now agree that collecting time statistics adds little, if anything, to database overhead, so setting *timed_statistics* to TRUE should not be a worry. The parameter can be dynamically altered at both the system and session levels, so the database does not have to be shut down and then restarted for the change to take effect. A simple *alter system set timed_statistics*=TRUE should do the trick.

The next prerequisite to using bottleneck analysis is that certain wait events should be filtered out of any metrics used to diagnose performance bottlenecks. For example, Oracle will record a wait statistic that represents how long a particular user sits at their SQL*Plus prompt between each issued database request.

Such a statistic provides no real value to a DBA who is trying to figure out where a database bottleneck exists. Any SQL scripts that are used to collect database wait statistics should exclude such events. A listing of these Oracle events, normally dubbed idle events, to eliminate includes:

- lock element cleanup
- PMON timer
- rdbms ipc message
- SMON timer
- SQL*Net message from client
- SQL*Net break/reset to client
- SQL*Net message to client
- SQL*Net more data to client
- dispatcher timer
- Null event
- parallel query dequeue wait
- parallel query idle wait - Slaves
- pipe get
- PL/SQL lock timer
- slave wait
- virtual circuit status

When collecting wait statistics, there are several levels of detail that can be penetrated. The first level is the system view, which provides a global, cumulative snapshot of all the waits that have occurred on a system. Viewing these numbers can help determine which wait events have caused the most commotion in a database thus far. A query that can be used to collect these metrics is the *syswaits.sql* script:

🖫 syswaits.sql

```
select
        event,
        total_waits,
        round(100 * (total_waits / sum_waits),2) pct_tot_waits,
        time_wait_sec,
        round(100 * (time_wait_sec / sum_secs),2) pct_secs_waits,
        total_timeouts,
        avg_wait_sec
from
(select
        event,
        total_waits,
        round((time_waited / 100),2) time_wait_sec,
        total_timeouts,
        round((average_wait / 100),2) avg_wait_sec
from
        sys.v_$system_event
where
        event not in
        ('lock element cleanup',
         'pmon timer',
         'rdbms ipc message',
         'smon timer',
         'SQL*Net message from client',
         'SQL*Net break/reset to client',
         'SQL*Net message to client',
         'SQL*Net more data to client',
         'dispatcher timer',
         'Null event',
         'parallel query dequeue wait',
         'parallel query idle wait - Slaves',
         'pipe get',
         'PL/SQL lock timer',
         'slave wait',
         'virtual circuit status',
         'WMON goes to sleep') and
        event not like 'DFS%' and
        event not like 'KXFX%'),
(select
        sum(total_waits) sum_waits,
        sum(round((time_waited / 100),2)) sum_secs
 from
        sys.v_$system_event
 where
        event not in
        ('lock element cleanup',
```

```
        'pmon timer',
        'rdbms ipc message',
        'smon timer',
        'SQL*Net message from client',
        'SQL*Net break/reset to client',
        'SQL*Net message to client',
        'SQL*Net more data to client',
        'dispatcher timer',
        'Null event',
        'parallel query dequeue wait',
        'parallel query idle wait - Slaves',
        'pipe get',
        'PL/SQL lock timer',
        'slave wait',
        'virtual circuit status',
        'WMON goes to sleep') and
        event not like 'DFS%' and
        event not like 'KXFX%')
order by
   2 desc;
```

	EVENT	TOTAL_WAITS	PCT_TOT_WAITS	TIME_WAIT_SEC	PCT_TIME_WAITS	TOTAL_TIMEOUTS	AVG_WAIT_SEC
1	control file parallel write	77154	64.69	67.18	37.74	0	0
2	direct path write	18271	15.32	28.54	16.03	0	0
3	control file sequential read	10531	8.83	24.74	13.9	0	0
4	direct path read	7758	6.5	34.86	19.58	0	0
5	db file sequential read	2627	2.2	5.33	2.99	0	0
6	refresh controlfile command	1401	1.17	10.94	6.15	0	.01
7	log file parallel write	477	.4	.45	.25	1	0
8	log file sync	276	.23	1.4	.79	0	.01
9	db file parallel write	266	.22	1.94	1.09	0	.01
10	file open	156	.13	.99	.56	0	.01
11	db file scattered read	125	.1	.11	.06	0	0
12	latch free	97	.08	1.11	.62	89	.01
13	file identify	47	.04	.18	.1	0	0
14	buffer busy waits	22	.02	.02	.01	0	0
15	library cache pin	21	.02	0	0	0	0
16	LGWR wait for redo copy	9	.01	.03	.02	3	0
17	rdbms ipc reply	7	.01	0	0	0	0
18	log file sequential read	5	0	0	0	0	0
19	log file single write	5	0	0	0	0	0
20	single-task message	5	0	.18	.1	0	.04
21	SQL*Net more data from client	4	0	0	0	0	0
22	reliable message	1	0	0	0	0	0
23	library cache load lock	1	0	0	0	0	0
24	instance state change	1	0	0	0	0	0

Figure 2.6: *Sample Output Showing System Waits*

But what is a db file sequential read anyway? Database file sequential reads normally indicate index lookup operations or ROWID fetches from a table. If the requested Oracle blocks are not already in memory, the initiating process must wait for them to be read in. Such activity seems to be the main source of contention in the above listing.

After looking at system-level wait activity, drill down further to discover which current connections may be responsible for any reported waits that are being observed at the system level. One query that can be used to collect such data is the *sesswaits.sql* script:

🖫 sesswaits.sql

```
select
      b.sid,
      decode(b.username,NULL,c.name,b.username) process_name,
      event,
      a.total_waits,
      round((a.time_waited / 100),2)
      time_wait_sec,a.total_timeouts,
      round((average_wait / 100),2)
      average_wait_sec,
      round((a.max_wait / 100),2) max_wait_sec
  from
      sys.v_$session_event a,
      sys.v_$session b,
      sys.v_$bgprocess c
  where
      event NOT IN
        ('lock element cleanup',
         'pmon timer',
         'rdbms ipc message',
         'smon timer',
         'SQL*Net message from client',
         'SQL*Net break/reset to client',
         'SQL*Net message to client',
         'SQL*Net more data to client',
         'dispatcher timer',
         'Null event',
         'parallel query dequeue wait',
         'parallel query idle wait - Slaves',
         'pipe get',
         'PL/SQL lock timer',
         'slave wait',
         'virtual circuit status',
         'WMON goes to sleep'
        )
  and event NOT LIKE 'DFS%'
  and event NOT LIKE 'KXFX%'
  and a.sid = b.sid
  and b.paddr = c.paddr (+)
order by
    4 desc;
```

	SID	PROCESS_NAME	EVENT	TOTAL_WAITS	TIME_WAIT_SEC	TOTAL_TIMEOUTS	AVERAGE_WAIT_SEC	MAX_WAIT_SEC
1	4	CKPT	control file parallel write	729	8.77	0	.01	.86
2	11	SYS	control file sequential read	262	2.54	0	.01	.14
3	4	CKPT	control file sequential read	228	10.31	0	.05	.23
4	5	SMON	db file scattered read	124	13.08	0	.11	.22
5	9	SCHED	db file sequential read	111	8.84	0	.08	.19
6	11	SYS	db file sequential read	73	3.69	0	.05	.15
7	3	LGWR	log file parallel write	69	1.92	64	.03	.13
8	5	SMON	db file sequential read	68	6.13	0	.09	.19
9	2	DBW0	control file sequential read	35	1.74	0	.05	.25
10	3	LGWR	control file sequential read	30	1.91	0	.06	.16
11	2	DBW0	direct path read	18	.22	0	.01	.15
12	2	DBW0	db file parallel write	16	.22	16	.01	.08
13	3	LGWR	control file parallel write	14	1.43	0	.1	.26
14	3	LGWR	direct path read	9	0	0	0	0
15	8	SYS	db file sequential read	8	.25	0	.03	.08
16	3	LGWR	direct path write	8	.17	0	.02	.17
17	3	LGWR	log file single write	7	.33	0	.05	.07
18	3	LGWR	log file sequential read	6	.22	0	.04	.07
19	9	SCHED	log file sync	3	.08	0	.03	.03
20	11	SYS	library cache pin	3	.12	0	.04	.12
21	2	DBW0	async disk IO	2	.22	0	.11	.15
22	3	LGWR	async disk IO	2	.17	0	.09	.17
23	11	SYS	buffer busy waits	1	.01	0	.01	.01
24	6	RECO	db file sequential read	1	.12	0	.12	.12

Figure 2.7: *Sample Historical Wait Output at the Session Level*

Such a query, for example, could indicate the Oracle processes responsible for most of the db file sequential waits that were reported in the global system overview query. Like the system-level query, the above query shows cumulative wait statistics for each session since it has been connected. Note that all data for that session is lost once it disconnects from the database.

A final level of detail can be obtained by checking for any active Oracle processes that are currently waiting. One query that can be used to uncover such data is the *csesswaits.sql* script:

💾 csesswaits.sql

```
select
        a.sid,
        decode(b.username,NULL,c.name,b.username) process_name,
        a.event,
        a.seconds_in_wait,
        a.wait_time,
        a.state,
        a.p1text,
        a.p1,
        a.p1raw,
        a.p2text,
        a.p2,
```

```
            a.p2raw,
            a.p3text,
            a.p3,
            a.p3raw
    from
            sys.v_$session_wait a,
            sys.v_$session b,
            sys.v_$bgprocess c
    where
            event NOT IN
                ('lock element cleanup',
                'pmon timer',
                'rdbms ipc message',
                'smon timer',
                'SQL*Net message from client',
                'SQL*Net break/reset to client',
                'SQL*Net message to client',
                'SQL*Net more data to client',
                'dispatcher timer',
                'Null event',
                'parallel query dequeue wait',
                'parallel query idle wait - Slaves',
                'pipe get',
                'PL/SQL lock timer',
                'slave wait',
                'virtual circuit status',
                'WMON goes to sleep'
                )
        and event NOT LIKE 'DFS%'
        and event NOT LIKE 'KXFX%'
        and a.sid = b.sid
        and b.paddr = c.paddr (+)
    order by
            4 desc;
```

	SID	PROCESS_NAME	EVENT	SECONDS_IN_WAIT	WAIT_TIME	STATE	P1TEXT	P1	P1RAW	P2TEXT	P2	P2RAW	P3TEXT	P3	P3RAW
1	10	ERADMIN	enqueue	3	0	WAITING	name|mode	1415053318	54580006	id1	524312	00080018	id2	31373	00007A8D

Figure 2.8: *Output Showing a Session Currently Waiting on a Resource*

If a current process is noticed with a db file sequential read wait, data contained in the parameter columns of the above query, i.e. p1text, p1, and such, can be used to locate the exact file and block of the object being used by Oracle to satisfy the end user's request.

If enqueue waits are found present when the output of current session waits is examined, use the *objwait.sql* script to find which object and datafile are causing the holdup:

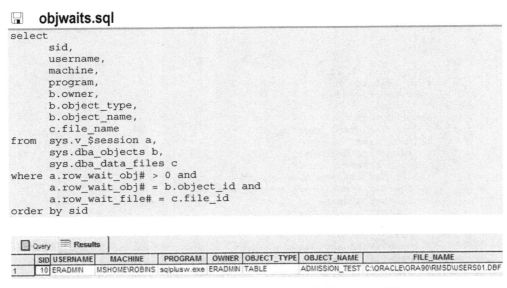

```
objwaits.sql

select
        sid,
        username,
        machine,
        program,
        b.owner,
        b.object_type,
        b.object_name,
        c.file_name
from    sys.v_$session a,
        sys.dba_objects b,
        sys.dba_data_files c
where   a.row_wait_obj# > 0 and
        a.row_wait_obj# = b.object_id and
        a.row_wait_file# = c.file_id
order by sid
```

	SID	USERNAME	MACHINE	PROGRAM	OWNER	OBJECT_TYPE	OBJECT_NAME	FILE_NAME
1	10	ERADMIN	MSHOME\ROBINS	sqlplusw.exe	ERADMIN	TABLE	ADMISSION_TEST	C:\ORACLE\ORA90\RMSD\USERS01.DBF

Figure 2.9: *Uncovering the Objects and Datafiles / Enqueue Wait*

When using bottleneck analysis, the information contained in the wait event views that Oracle provides is not the only thing that can be relied on. For example, an object may attempt to extend into another extent of space in a tablespace, and yet be denied if no such free space exists.

Such a failure will not be reflected in any wait event but still represents a very real bottleneck to the database. In the same way that only a few ratios cannot be depended on to properly carry out ratio-based performance analysis, an administrator must include several statistical metrics in their overall bottleneck analysis framework to obtain an accurate performance-risk assessment.

For example, in the aforementioned object extension failure, the DBA would want to include a query in her bottleneck analysis framework that returns a count of any object that has reached, or better yet, approaches its maximum extent limit or is housed in a tablespace with insufficient free space to accommodate its next extent. Now that each method has been reviewed, examine an effective approach that combines bottleneck and ratio analysis techniques.

Combining Bottleneck and Ratio Analysis

To provide the best possible coverage for a database, it is best to utilize both ratio-based and bottleneck analysis in their performance-monitoring toolkit. While there are many ways to accomplish this, one approach is to categorize each area of performance interest, and then list out the metrics that should be used for both ratio-based and bottleneck analysis.

Realize that some ratio-based metrics can be represented as bottleneck metrics and vice-versa; for example, while a ratio could be used to indicate how full an Oracle archive log destination has become, such a measure could also be used as a bottleneck metric that represents an approaching space-related blockage, and some metrics can overlap categories. To summarize the strength and weakness of each approach:

Performance Area: Memory

Ratio-Based Metrics	Bottleneck-Based Metrics
Buffer Cache Hit Ratio	Buffer Busy
Data Dictionary Cache Hit Ratio	Enqueue Waits
Free Shared Pool Percent	Free Buffer Waits
Library Cache Hit Ratio	Latch Free Waits
Memory/Disk Sort Ratio	Library Cache Pin Waits
Parse/Execute Ratio	Library Cache Load Lock
Leading Memory Session Percentage	Waits
	Log Buffer Space Waits
	Library Object Reloads Count
	Redo Log Space Waits
	Redo Log Space Wait Time

Table 2.1: *Ratio-Based Metrics to Bottleneck-Based Metrics*

Troubleshooting SQL Execution

There is a need to be able to quickly pinpoint resource-intensive SQL code that is causing undo strain on the database. Understanding current and historical SQL execution patterns will enable the second set of data necessary to properly perform workload analysis.

Keep in mind that while locating SQL calls that are racking up expensive statistics is not hard since it is an integral part of all STATSPACK and AWR reports, the actual process of optimizing SQL can be quite complicated. While there are third-party software products that can help in rewriting SQL queries, one will not be found that will tell that a particular SQL statement should not be executed. Only by understanding a particular application's needs can this be accomplished. Removing SQL waste in a database can produce dramatic results as, believe it or not, sometimes the best SQL query is the one that is not executed.

Using a singular diagnostic approach to database performance analysis may, under the right conditions, result in pinpointing a database slowdown, but a more holistic approach is to utilize metrics and collection methods from both ratio-based and bottleneck analysis, as well as techniques found in workload analysis. As with investing in the stock market, a person might not be right every time, but they can limit most losses by staying true to a combined and proven methodology.

Summary

Several specific database issues were covered in Chapter 2 with focus on reactive methods such as wait event analysis and trace dump analysis. Additional attention was given to ratio-based analysis and bottleneck analysis. The buffer cache hit ratio (BCHR) tool was also examined in detail as well as the data buffer cache advisory. The next chapter deals with database performance.

Troubleshooting Database Performance

The Number One Oracle Performance Myth

Whether it is in the realm of database technology or any other discipline, some maxims are whispered around the campfire so much that they are taken for gospel at face value and never questioned, especially when supposed experts mouth the words. Such is the case with a database performance myth that has been around for as long as most can remember. It goes something like this:

"Eighty percent of a database's overall performance is derived from the code that is written against it."

This is a complete untruth, or at the very least, an overestimation of the impact that properly written SQL code has against a running physical database. Good coding practices definitely count, often heavily, toward the success of any database application, but to state affirmatively that they make a contribution of over two-thirds is a stretch.

The reason this proverb cannot pass the reality test is that it is stated independently of what good or bad code can do in the face of poor physical design. The real world case that opened this book is a shining example of how wrong this adage is.

The physical design constrains all code - good or bad - and has the capability to turn even the best-written SQL into molasses. After all, how can a SQL developer obtain unique key index access unless the physical index has been created and is in place?

How can a database coder scan only the parts of a table that they need unless that table has been partitioned to accommodate such a request? Only when a solid physical design is put in place, a design that fits the application like a glove, can SQL code really take off and make for some impressive response times. Remember, good design comes first.

What about the link between availability and design? According to Oracle Corporation's own studies of client downtime, the largest percentage, up to 36%, are design-related issues. If database design has not been considered a serious issue until now, consider this a wake-up call.

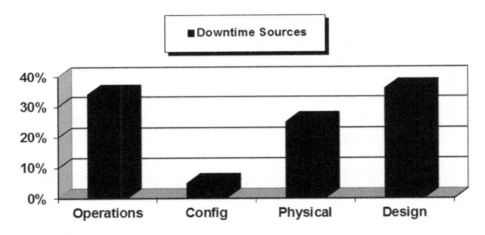

Figure 3.1: *Downtime Statistics Provide by Oracle Corporation*

Troubleshooting Oracle Disk Performance

If the reason that most DBAs' pagers go off at night could be tracked, it would be a fair bet to say that a leading cause would be storage-related problems. However, the good news is that this does not have to be the case if proactive techniques are used.

Automatic Growth

Way back in version 7, Oracle introduced the concept of auto-extendable datafiles. This simple addition to Oracle has silenced many a DBA's pager. It basically allows Oracle to automatically grow a datafile to meet the need of incoming or changed data if not enough free space currently exists in the tablespace. To enable this feature, either create a tablespace with autoextend enabled or alter a tablespace after creation to turn the feature on. An example of creating a tablespace with autoextend initially enabled would be:

```
create tablespace
   users
datafile
   'd:\oracle\ora92\o92\users01.dbf' size 25600k
autoextend on next 1280k maxsize unlimited
extent management local autoallocate
logging
online;
```

Some DBAs have an aversion to using autoextend and instead prefer to preallocate space to a tablespace. If proper capacity planning measures are used, this approach can work just fine. However, if the database is very dynamic and unpredictable, then autoextend should be enabled for most tablespaces, especially temporary tablespaces that can be the object of large sort operations.

Some DBAs may not know whether autoextend is enabled for their tablespaces and datafiles. Furthermore, they may not know how much total space their storage structures are currently taking up. Depending on the Oracle version being used, one of the two following scripts can give these exact facts.

🖫 spacesum.sql

```
select
      tablespace_name,
      autoextend,
      round ((total_space / 1024 / 1024), 2) as
      total_space,
      round ((total_free_space /
      1024 / 1024), 2) as total_free,
      round (((total_space - total_free_space) /
```

```
            1024 / 1024), 2) as used_space,
        to_char (
            nvl (
                round (
                    (100 *
                        sum_free_blocks /
                        sum_alloc_blocks),2),0)) || '%'
                as pct_free
    from (select
                tablespace_name,
                max (autoextensible) autoextend,
                sum (blocks) sum_alloc_blocks,
                sum (bytes) as total_space
            from
                dba_data_files
            group by tablespace_name),
        (select
                b.tablespace_name fs_ts_name,
                nvl (sum (bytes), 0) as total_free_space,
                sum (blocks) as sum_free_blocks
            from
                dba_free_space a, dba_tablespaces b
            where
                a.tablespace_name (+) = b.tablespace_name
            group by b.tablespace_name,   status)
        tablespace_name = fs_ts_name
union all
select
        d.tablespace_name, autoextend,
        round ((a.bytes / 1024 / 1024), 2),
        round ((a.bytes / 1024 / 1024) -
        (nvl (t.bytes, 0) / 1024 / 1024), 2),
        round (nvl (t.bytes, 0) / 1024 / 1024, 2),
        to_char (100 - (nvl (t.bytes /
        a.bytes * 100, 0)), '990.00')
    from
        sys.dba_tablespaces d,
        (select
                tablespace_name,
                max (autoextensible) autoextend,
                sum (bytes) bytes
            from
                dba_temp_files
            group by tablespace_name) a,
        (select
                tablespace_name, sum (bytes_cached) bytes
            from
                sys.v_$temp_extent_pool
            group by tablespace_name) t
    where
        d.tablespace_name = a.tablespace_name (+)
    and d.tablespace_name = t.tablespace_name (+)
    and d.extent_management like 'LOCAL'
    and d.contents like 'TEMPORARY'
order by 1;
```

	TABLESPACE_NAME	AUTOEXTEND	TOTAL_SPACE	TOTAL_FREE	USED_SPACE	PCT_FREE
1	AUTOSEG	NO	5	4.94	.06	98.75%
2	DRSYS	YES	20	15.19	4.81	75.94%
3	INDX	YES	25	24.88	.13	99.5%
4	OEM_REPOSITORY	YES	35.01	3	32.01	8.57%
5	SYSTEM	YES	300	3.63	296.38	1.21%
6	TEMP	YES	556	1	555	0.18
7	TOOLS	YES	10	7.75	2.25	77.5%
8	UNDOTBS1	YES	210	208.69	1.31	99.38%
9	USERS	YES	25	15.13	9.88	60.5%
10	XDB	YES	38.13	.19	37.94	.49%

Figure 3.2: *Output Displaying Summary Space Information and Autoextend Properties for Tablespaces*

While the queries above will let the DBA know if a tablespace has autoextend enabled, it will not tell which datafile if the tablespace has multiple datafiles. For that, he will need the *datafileae.sql* script, which will work for all Oracle versions:

datafileae.sql

```
select
       b.file_name,
       b.tablespace_name,
       decode(c.inc,null,'no','yes') autoextend
  from
       sys.dba_data_files b,
       sys.filext$ c
where
       c.file# (+)= b.file_id
order by
       2, 1;
```

	FILE_NAME	TABLESPACE_NAME	AUTOEXTEND
1	D:\ORACLE\ORA92\O92\AUTOSEG.ORA	AUTOSEG	NO
2	D:\ORACLE\ORA92\O92\DRSYS01.DBF	DRSYS	YES
3	D:\ORACLE\ORA92\O92\INDX01.DBF	INDX	YES
4	D:\ORACLE\ORA92\O92\OEM_REPOSITORY.DBF	OEM_REPOSITORY	YES
5	D:\ORACLE\ORA92\O92\SYSTEM01.DBF	SYSTEM	YES
6	D:\ORACLE\ORA92\O92\TOOLS01.DBF	TOOLS	YES
7	D:\ORACLE\ORA92\O92\UNDOTBS01.DBF	UNDOTBS1	YES
8	D:\ORACLE\ORA92\O92\USERS01.DBF	USERS	YES
9	D:\ORACLE\ORA92\O92\XDB01.DBF	XDB	YES

Figure 3.3: *Information Regarding What Datafiles Have Autoextend Enabled*

The last thing to keep in mind regarding objects with unlimited extents is that it is still possible for an object not to be able to extend, even if it has an unlimited extent limit. The three primary reasons an object will fail to extend include:

- No file autoextend: The tablespace that the object resides in does not have autoextend enabled, and there is not enough room in the tablespace to add the object's new extent.

- No filesystem space: The tablespace that the object resides in has autoextend enabled, but the drive/file system that the tablespace is on is out of free space and will not allow the tablespace to automatically grow.

- Fragmentation problem: The dictionary managed tablespace that the object resides in has enough total free space to add the object's new extent, but the free space is not contiguous in nature because of bubble fragmentation, and therefore, the object cannot extend,

Troubleshooting Critical Storage Problems

As much as possible, it is best to adopt a proactive approach to Oracle storage management. Naturally, the first step in this is ensuring that the current and future space needs of the database are intelligently planned for, both inside the database and outside on the server, and all the ammunition that Oracle provides with respect to space-related features is being used.

While this is all well and good for new databases, an existing database may be inherited that is not in tiptop shape from a storage standpoint. What sort of investigating should be done on such databases to determine their storage health, and how should any new databases be kept free from space-related headaches?

Detecting Tablespace Fragmentation

How can a DBA tell if the tablespaces are suffering from fragmentation problems and then identify the type of fragmentation? The detection and diagnosis is not hard to make at all. To determine if the tablespaces are having a problem with fragmentation, use the *tsfrag.sql* script:

🖫 **tsfrag.sql**

```
select
        tablespace_name,
        count(*) free_chunks,
        decode(round((max(bytes) / 1024000),2),null,0,
        round((max(bytes) / 1024000),2)) largest_chunk,
        nvl(round(sqrt(max(blocks)/sum(blocks))*
    (100/sqrt(sqrt(count(blocks)) )),2),0)
        fragmentation_index
from
        sys.dba_free_space
group by
        tablespace_name
order by
        2 desc, 1;
```

	TABLESPACE_NAME	FREE_CHUNKS	LARGEST_CHUNK	FRAGMENTATION_INDEX
1	TEMP	2208	.44	.81
2	USER_DATA	73	63.23	31.33
3	RBS	36	18.94	15.77
4	USER_DATA2	8	4.66	57.06
5	ER_DATA	5	2.47	47.33
6	BROKER_DATA	3	8.26	72.94
7	BROKER_INDEXES	1	10.18	100
8	OEM_REPOSITORY	1	2.82	100
9	USER_DATA3	1	12.28	100
10	SYSTEM	1	.24	100
11	TEST	1	1.02	100
12	TEST_TS	1	14.27	100
13	TOOLS	1	5.08	100
14	USER_INDEXES	1	.38	100

Figure 3.4: *Checking for Tablespace Fragmentation*

When the script output is examined, hone in on a couple of columns in particular. First, notice the fragmentation index column. This will give the tablespace an overall ranking with respect to how badly it is actually fragmented. A 100% score indicates no fragmentation at all. Lesser scores verify the presence of fragmentation.

The free chunks count column will tell how many segments of free space are scattered throughout the tablespace. One thing to keep in mind is that tablespaces with multiple datafiles will always show a free chunk count greater than one because each datafile will likely have at least one pocket of free space.

To drill down a little further and find out how badly fragmented each datafile in the database is, use the *dffrag.sql* script:

dffrag.sql

```
select
      b.file_name, b.tablespace_name,
      nvl(round(sqrt(max(a.blocks)/
      sum(a.blocks))*(100/sqrt(sqrt(count(a.blocks)) )),2),0)
      fragmentation_index,
      decode(c.inc,null,'no','yes') autoextend,
```

```
        count (*) free_chunks,
        decode (
            round ((max (a.bytes) / 1024000), 2),
            null, 0,
            round ((max (a.bytes) / 1024000), 2)) largest_chunk
  from
        sys.dba_free_space a,
        sys.dba_data_files b,
        sys.filext$ c
 where
        b.tablespace_name = a.tablespace_name (+) and
        c.file# (+)= a.file_id and
        b.file_id = a.file_id (+)
group
        by b.file_name,
        decode(c.inc,null,'no','yes'),
        b.tablespace_name
 order
        by 5 desc, 1;
```

	FILE_NAME	TABLESPACE_NAME	FRAGMENTATION_INDEX	AUTOEXTEND	FREE_CHUNKS	LARGEST_CHUNK
1	D:\ORACLE\ORADATA\O817\TEMP01.DBF	TEMP	.81	YES	2208	.44
2	D:\ORACLE\ORADATA\O817\USERS01.DBF	USER_DATA	32.08	YES	68	63.23
3	D:\ORACLE\ORADATA\O817\RBS01.DBF	RBS	15.77	YES	36	18.94
4	D:\ORACLE\ORADATA\O817\USER_DATA2.DBF	USER_DATA2	57.06	NO	8	4.66
5	D:\ORACLE\ORADATA\O817\ER_DATA.DBF	ER_DATA	47.33	NO	5	2.47
6	D:\ORACLE\ORADATA\O817\USERS02.DBF	USER_DATA	43.98	YES	5	.38
7	D:\ORACLE\ORADATA\O817\BROKER_DATA.DBF	BROKER_DATA	72.94	YES	3	8.26
8	D:\ORACLE\ORADATA\O817\BIGADMIN.DBF	BIG_ADMISSION	0	NO	1	0
9	D:\ORACLE\ORADATA\O817\BROKER_INDEXES.DBF	BROKER_INDEXES	100	YES	1	10.18
10	D:\ORACLE\ORADATA\O817\INDX01.DBF	USER_INDEXES	100	YES	1	.38
11	D:\ORACLE\ORADATA\O817\OEM_REPOSITORY.ORA	OEM_REPOSITORY	100	YES	1	2.82
12	D:\ORACLE\ORADATA\O817\USER_DATA3.DBF	USER_DATA3	100	NO	1	12.28
13	D:\ORACLE\ORADATA\O817\SYSTEM01.DBF	SYSTEM	100	YES	1	.24
14	D:\ORACLE\ORADATA\O817\TEST01.DBF	TEST	100	YES	1	1.02
15	D:\ORACLE\ORADATA\O817\TEST_TS.ORA	TEST_TS	100	YES	1	14.27
16	D:\ORACLE\ORADATA\O817\TOOLS01.DBF	TOOLS	100	YES	1	5.08

Figure 3.5: *Checking for Datafile Fragmentation*

One last thing to remember in detecting tablespace fragmentation is that even if numerous free chunk counts are found in locally- managed tablespaces, it really is not an issue.

Since every object placed in the tablespace will have the same extent size, sooner or later the pockets of free space will be reused whether new objects are placed into the tablespace or existing objects extend. If fragmentation is indeed found in the tablespaces, identify whether it is of the honeycomb or bubble variety.

To answer this question, produce a tablespace map that plots the entire tablespace in datafile/block ID order. Doing so will show a number of interesting things including where the actual objects in the tablespace reside along with where the pockets of free space are located. A clean tablespace will normally show one large segment of free space at the end. A badly fragmented tablespace will show bubbles of free space interspersed throughout. Two free space segments that reside next to one another can identify honeycombs.

tsmap.sql

```
select
        'free space' object_owner,
        '    ' object_type,
        '    ' object_name,
        file_id,
        block_id,
        bytes / 1024 size_kb,
        blocks
from
        sys.dba_free_space
where
        tablespace_name = <:tablespace name>
union all
select
        owner,
        segment_type,
        decode (partition_name,null,segment_name,segment_name ||
        '.' || partition_name),
        file_id,
        block_id,
        bytes / 1024,
        blocks
from
        sys.dba_extents
where
        tablespace_name = <:tablespace name>
order by
        4,5;
```

	OBJECT_OWNER	OBJECT_TYPE	OBJECT_NAME	FILE_ID	BLOCK_ID	SIZE_KB	BLOCKS
1	USER21	TABLE	TAB1	3	2	128	16
2	ERADMIN	INDEX	PK22	3	18	128	16
3	free space			3	34	128	16
4	USER21	TABLE	INDEX1	3	50	128	16
5	EMBT_CP	INDEX	REF61	3	66	128	16
6	EMBT_CP	INDEX	REF63	3	82	128	16
7	EMBT_CP	INDEX	REF62	3	98	128	16
8	free space			3	114	128	16
9	ERADMIN	LOBSEGMENT	SYS_LOB0000034196C00001$$	3	130	128	16
10	free space			3	146	128	16
11	EMBT_CP	TABLE	CP_TABLE	3	162	128	16
12	EMBT_CP	INDEX	REF67	3	178	128	16
13	ERADMIN	TABLE	TEST_RAW	3	194	128	16
14	BILLY	TABLE	PLAN_TABLE	3	210	128	16
15	ERADMIN	TABLE	EMP_BKP	3	226	128	16
16	ERADMIN	TABLE	CREATE$JAVA$LOB$TABLE	3	242	128	16
17	BAD_GUY	TABLE	ROB	3	258	128	16
18	ERADMIN	TABLE	DOCTOR_PROCEDURE	3	274	128	16
19	ERADMIN	INDEX	PK10	3	290	128	16
20	ERADMIN	TABLE	EMPLOYEE	3	306	128	16
21	ERADMIN	TABLE	MEDICATION	3	322	128	16
22	ERADMIN	INDEX	PK11	3	338	128	16
23	ERADMIN	TABLE	MEDICATION_DISP	3	354	128	16
24	ERADMIN	INDEX	PK12	3	370	128	16
25	ERADMIN	TABLE	MEDICATION_DISPM	3	386	128	16
26	ERADMIN	INDEX	PK13	3	402	128	16
27	ERADMIN	TABLE	NURSE	3	418	128	16
28	ERADMIN	LOBINDEX	SYS_IL0000034102C00002$$	3	434	128	16

Figure 3.6: *Mapping the Contents of a Tablespace*

Detecting Object Fragmentation

Object fragmentation can damage the performance in one of two ways: First, if there are objects in dictionary-managed tablespaces that have a maximum extent limit set to something other than unlimited, then the objects could run out of space.

As a result of repeated insert and delete activity, tables can become internally fragmented and contain a lot of wasted space. In the same way, indexes can become fragmented so that their depth reaches unacceptable levels. This predicament will be covered in the next section.

How to tell if the objects are getting close to hitting their maximum extent limit? This is quite easy to do. If version 7 of Oracle is being used, then execute the *maxext7.sql* script, which will find all objects that are within five extents of their limit:

💾 maxext.sql

```
select
      owner,
      decode(partition_name,NULL,segment_name,segment_name ||
      '.' || partition_name) segment_name,
      segment_type,
      extents,
      max_extents,
      initial_extent,
      next_extent,
      tablespace_name
from
      sys.dba_segments
where
      max_extents - extents <= 5 and
      segment_type <> 'CACHE'
order by
      1,2,3;
```

	OWNER	SEGMENT_NAME	SEGMENT_TYPE	EXTENTS	MAX_EXTENTS	INITIAL_EXTENT	NEXT_EXTENT	TABLESPACE_NAME
1	ERADMIN	CANT_EXTEND	TABLE	3	4	131072	131072	USER_DATA
2	USER21	TABLE1	TABLE	1	1	16384	6144000	USER_DATA
3	USER21	TABLE2	TABLE	1	1	106496	8192	USER_DATA
4	USER21	TABLE3	TABLE	1	1	106496	8192	USER_DATA

Figure 3.7: *Output Showing Objects Nearing Their Maximum Extent Limit*

Second, an extent problem arises when an object in a dictionary-managed tablespace cannot extend because of a lack of contiguous free space. To uncover these types of problems, use the *objdef.sql* script:

💾 objdef.sql

```
select
    a.owner,
    a.segment_name,
    a.segment_type,
    a.tablespace_name,
    a.next_extent,
    max(c.bytes) max_contig_space
from
    sys.dba_segments a,
    sys.dba_free_space c
where
    a.tablespace_name = c.tablespace_name and
    a.next_extent >
      (select
            max(bytes)
```

```
        from
                sys.dba_free_space b
        where
                a.tablespace_name = b.tablespace_name and
                b.tablespace_name = c.tablespace_name)
group by
        a.owner,
        a.segment_name,
        a.tablespace_name,
        a.segment_type,
        a.next_extent
```

	OWNER	SEGMENT_NAME	SEGMENT_TYPE	TABLESPACE_NAME	NEXT_EXTENT	MAX_CONTIG_SPACE
1	BAD_GUY	ADMISSION	TABLE PARTITION	USER_DATA	104857600	64749568
2	ERADMIN	ADMISSION	TABLE PARTITION	USER_DATA	104857600	64749568
3	ERADMIN	REF440	INDEX	USER_DATA	102400000	64749568
4	USER21	TABLE1	TABLE	USER_DATA	6144000	4767744
5	SYS	C_FILE#_BLOCK#	CLUSTER	SYSTEM	335872	245760
6	SYS	EMBARCADERO_EXPLAIN_PLAN	TABLE	SYSTEM	507904	245760
7	SYS	I_IDL_SB41	INDEX	SYSTEM	335872	245760
8	SYS	I_IDL_UB11	INDEX	SYSTEM	1146880	245760
9	SYS	I_IDL_UB21	INDEX	SYSTEM	335872	245760
10	SYS	JAVANM	TABLE	SYSTEM	507904	245760

Figure 3.8: *Output Showing Objects That Have a Space Deficit in Their Parent Tablespace*

Correcting Object Fragmentation

The prescription for correcting object fragmentation is generally total object reorganization. Such a procedure used to be fraught with errors and fear, even when third party software products were used. Fortunately, this is not really the case any longer as Oracle has provided more built-in reorganization capabilities with each new release. Oracle has even gone so far as to grant online reorganization abilities for certain object types.

The next section will cover in detail the reorganization techniques and methods that can be used to fix the objects when it is discovered that they need to be reorganized.

Troubleshooting Table Problems

Needless to say, tables that suffer from high levels of wasted space could definitely be causing the database to spin in ways that are not wanted.

The other problem that might exist in the tables is one of chained/migrated rows. Under normal circumstances, a row of data should fit completely inside one Oracle block. Sometimes, however, this is not the case, and the table suddenly finds itself containing chained or migrated rows, which are rows that span more than one data block.

Chaining occurs when a row is initially too large to fit inside one block. Two or more blocks are used by Oracle to hold the row. Migration deals with rows that have grown so much that they can no longer be contained within their original block. When this occurs, Oracle relocates the row out of its original block into another block, but leaves a pointer behind to indicate the relocation. Both chaining and migration force Oracle to perform more than one I/O to retrieve data that could normally be obtained with a single I/O operation. The end result is degraded performance.

How can the levels of wasted space be determined in the tables as well as finding out if they suffer from a chained/migrated row problem? The scripts below will provide all the answers that should be needed. They locate tables that contain 25% or more wasted space. As a bonus, the scripts also calculate the chained row ratio for a table, the percentage of used extents to maximum extents, and determine if the object can extend into its next block of free space.

In other words, these are nice reorganization diagnostic scripts.

🖫 tabreorg.sql

```
select
        /*+ RULE */
        owner,
        segment_name table_name,
        segment_type,
        round(bytes/1024,2) table_kb,
        num_rows,
        blocks,
        empty_blocks,
        hwm highwater_mark,
        avg_used_blocks,
        greatest(round(100 * (nvl(hwm - avg_used_blocks,0) /
        greatest(nvl(hwm,1),1) ),2),0) block_inefficiency,
        chain_pct,
        max_extent_pct,
```

```
        extents,
        max_extents,
        decode(greatest(max_free_space -
        next_extent,0),0,'n','y') can_extend_space,
        next_extent,
        max_free_space,
        o_tablespace_name tablespace_name
from
(select
        a.owner owner,
        segment_name,
        segment_type,
        bytes,
        num_rows,
        a.blocks blocks,
        b.empty_blocks empty_blocks,
        a.blocks - b.empty_blocks - 1 hwm,
        decode(round((b.avg_row_len * num_rows *
        (1 + (pct_free/100))) /
        c.blocksize,0),0,1,round((b.avg_row_len * num_rows *
        (1 + (pct_free/100))) / c.blocksize,0)) + 2
        avg_used_blocks,
        round(100 * (nvl(b.chain_cnt,0) /
        greatest(nvl(b.num_rows,1),1)),2)
        chain_pct,
        a.extents extents,
        round(100 * (a.extents / a.max_extents),2) max_extent_pct,
        a.max_extents max_extents,
        b.next_extent next_extent,
        b.tablespace_name o_tablespace_name
   from
        sys.dba_segments a,
        sys.dba_all_tables b,
        sys.ts$ c
  where
        ( a.owner = b.owner ) and
        ( segment_name = table_name ) and
        ( ( segment_type = 'TABLE ) ) and
        b.tablespace_name = c.name
union all
select
        a.owner owner,
        segment_name || '.' || b.partition_name,
        segment_type,
        bytes,
        b.num_rows,
        a.blocks blocks,
        b.empty_blocks empty_blocks,
        a.blocks - b.empty_blocks - 1 hwm,
        decode(round((b.avg_row_len * b.num_rows * (1 +
        (b.pct_free/100))) /
        c.blocksize,0),0,1,round((b.avg_row_len * b.num_rows *
        (1 + (b.pct_free/100))) / c.blocksize,0)) + 2
        avg_used_blocks,
        round(100 * (nvl(b.chain_cnt,0) /
        greatest(nvl(b.num_rows,1),1)),2)
        chain_pct,
        a.extents extents,
        round(100 * (a.extents / a.max_extents),2) max_extent_pct,
```

```
        a.max_extents max_extents,
        b.next_extent,
        b.tablespace_name o_tablespace_name
   from
        sys.dba_segments a,
        sys.dba_tab_partitions b,
        sys.ts$ c,
        sys.dba_tables d
   where
        ( a.owner = b.table_owner ) and
        ( segment_name = b.table_name ) and
        ( ( segment_type = TABLE PARTITION' ) ) and
        b.tablespace_name = c.name and
        d.owner = b.table_owner and
        d.table_name = b.table_name and
        a.partition_name = b.partition_name),
( select
        tablespace_name f_tablespace_name,
     max(bytes) max_free_space
   from
        sys.dba_free_space
   group by tablespace_name)
   where
        f_tablespace_name = o_tablespace_name and
        greatest(round(100 * (nvl(hwm - avg_used_blocks,0) /
        greatest(nvl(hwm,1),1) ),2),0) > 25
order by 10 desc, 1 asc,2 asc
```

	OWNER	TABLE_NAME	SEGMENT_TYPE	TABLE_KB	NUM_ROWS	BLOCKS	EMPTY_BLOCKS	HIGHWATER_MARK	AVG_USED_BLOCKS	BLOCK_INEFFICIENCY	CHAIN_PCT
1	ERADMIN	EMP	TABLE	19072	0	2384	120	2263	3	99.87	0
2	SYS	OBJ$	TABLE	2440	4387	305	1	303	43	85.81	0
3	SYS	ADMISSION_NO	TABLE	256	1520	32	0	31	5	83.87	0
4	USER21	TABLE1	TABLE	256	0	32	15	16	3	81.25	0
5	USER21	TABLE2	TABLE	256	130	32	12	19	4	78.95	0
6	USER21	TABLE3	TABLE	176	40	22	0	21	11	47.62	82.5
7	ERADMIN	EMBARCADERO	TABLE	384	2217	48	6	41	27	34.15	0
8	SYS	PROCEDURE$	TABLE	80	418	10	3	6	4	33.33	0
9	BRKADMIN	INVESTMENT	TABLE	64	412	8	0	7	5	28.57	0

Figure 3.9: *Partial Output Showing the Wasted Space Amounts and Chained Row Percentage of Database Tables*

If a DBA wants to see the shape that all his database tables are in, then he can remove the WHERE clause that restricts the output to only those tables having a block efficiency ranking of 25% or higher.

There are a couple of columns in Figure 3.9 that should be honed in on. The block inefficiency ranking will highlight any table that suffers from a lot of wasted space. For example, the *eradmin.emp* table has no rows in it but sports a very high watermark. Therefore, it tops the list in terms of tables with high amounts of wasted space. Also, notice the chain percent column. This column indicates how badly the table suffers from chained or migrated rows. In Figure 3.9, the *user21.table3* table appears to be in bad shape with respect to chained/migrated rows. Generally, if a table appears to have a chain percent of 25% or more, then it would be worthwhile to reorganize it.

Index Diagnostics

Like tables, indexes can become disorganized due to heavy DML activity. There has been much debate in the DBA world as to what a DBA should look for when determining if an index is in poor shape, but the script below should help. The script displays the level and clustering factor of the index, calculates the percentage of used extents to maximum extents, and also determines if the index can extend into its next block of free space.

🖫 **idxreorg.sql**

```
select
        /*+ RULE */
        owner,
        segment_name index_name,
        segment_type,
        round(bytes/1024,2) index_kb,
        num_rows,
        clustering_factor,
        blevel,
        blocks,
        max_extent_pct,
        extents,
        max_extents,
        decode(greatest(max_free_space -
        next_extent,0),0,'n','y') can_extend_space,
        next_extent,
        max_free_space,
        o_tablespace_name
from
(select
        a.owner owner,
        segment_name,
        segment_type,
        bytes,
        num_rows,
        b.clustering_factor,
        b.blevel,
        a.blocks blocks,
        a.extents extents,
        round(100 * (a.extents / a.max_extents),2)
        max_extent_pct,
```

```
        a.max_extents max_extents,
        b.next_extent next_extent,
        b.tablespace_name o_tablespace_name
    from
        sys.dba_segments a,
        sys.dba_indexes b,
        sys.ts$ c
  where
        ( a.owner = b.owner ) and
        ( segment_name = index_name ) and
        ( ( segment_type = 'INDEX' ) ) and
        b.tablespace_name = c.name
union all
select
        a.owner owner,
        segment_name || '.' || b.partition_name,
        segment_type,
        bytes,
        b.num_rows,
        b.clustering_factor,
        b.blevel,
        a.blocks blocks,
        a.extents extents,
        round(100 * (a.extents / a.max_extents),2)
        max_extent_pct,
        a.max_extents max_extents,
        b.next_extent,
        b.tablespace_name o_tablespace_name
    from
        sys.dba_segments a,
        sys.dba_ind_partitions b,
        sys.ts$ c,
        sys.dba_indexes d
  where
        ( a.owner = b.index_owner ) and
        ( segment_name = b.index_name ) and
        ( ( segment_type = INDEX PARTITION' ) ) and
        b.tablespace_name = c.name and
        d.owner = b.index_owner and
        d.index_name = b.index_name and
        a.partition_name = b.partition_name),
( select
        tablespace_name f_tablespace_name,
        max(bytes) max_free_space
    from
        sys.dba_free_space
    group by tablespace_name)
where
    f_tablespace_name = o_tablespace_name
order
    by 1,2;
```

Query | Results

	OWNER	INDEX_NAME	SEGMENT_TYPE	INDEX_KB	NUM_ROWS	CLUSTERING_FACTOR	BLEVEL	BLOCKS	MAX_EXTENT_PCT	EXTE
7	AURORAJISUTILITY$	SNS$NODE_INDEX	INDEX	64	84	10	0	8	0	
8	AURORAJISUTILITY$	SNS$PERM_INDEX	INDEX	64	312	1	0	8	0	
9	AURORAJISUTILITY$	SNS$REFADDR_INDEX	INDEX	64	291	5	0	8	0	
10	AURORAJISUTILITY$	SNS$SHARED$OBJ_INDEX	INDEX	64	0	0	0	8	0	
11	AURORAJISUTILITY$	SYS_C0011031	INDEX	64	117	1	0	8	0	
12	AURORAJISUTILITY$	SYS_C0011032	INDEX	64	0	0	0	8	0	
13	BILLY	SYS_C0011859	INDEX	128	0	0	0	16	.02	
14	BILLY	SYS_C0011860	INDEX	128	1	1	0	16	.02	
15	BRKADMIN	BROKER_COMMISSION_N1	INDEX	32	0	0	0	4	0	
16	BRKADMIN	BROKER_N1	INDEX	32	20	1	0	4	0	
17	BRKADMIN	CLIENT_N1	INDEX	32	500	8	0	4	0	

Figure 3.10: *Partial Output Showing Index Reorganization Diagnostics*

Seeing index levels beyond four, or bad clustering factors for indexes with supposed high cardinality, should lead to an investigation as to whether the index should be reorganized or even maintained in the system.

Correcting Space-related Object Performance Problems

While use of locally-managed tablespaces can just about make full tablespace reorganizations a thing of the past, object reorganizations are still necessary to remove headaches like wasted table space, chained/migrated table rows, deep index levels and more.

Oracle used to leave reorganization capabilities to third party software vendors, but newer versions of the RDBMS engine provide a number of built-in features that allow performing object reorganizations with simple DDL commands or packages.

Now look at the other side of the I/O spectrum: RAM.

Troubleshooting Memory Problems

When the subject of Oracle performance tuning comes up, almost every database professional thinks of tweaking the RAM memory settings. After all, is it not true that servers with more RAM run faster than comparable servers with less memory? Should not databases work the same?

Not surprisingly, the general answer is yes. Databases operating with more memory will usually run hundreds of times faster than those whose RAM allocations are rationed out in smaller portions. There are, of course, exceptions to every rule, and those will be covered in this book.

Those who think that throwing memory at a database is always going to solve serious performance problems are setting themselves up for a rude awakening. It takes a careful blend of balance and investigation to determine exactly how much memory a database needs and where those allocations should be made. It is also critically important not to over-allocate a database's memory allotment. Doing so can cause a server to page swap and thrash to a point where all operations come to a complete standstill.

Without a doubt, a small book could be written on the subject of memory concepts and tuning within Oracle. Instead of trying to cover every nook and cranny with respect to memory optimization, this book focuses on getting the most bang for the buck when the DBA begins to turn Oracle's memory knobs.

There is nothing more irritating than spending an hour and a half reading an in-depth white paper on something like Oracle latch analysis, and then discovering that following the author's advice yields no noticeable benefit on the database.

To be covered is information that should give the reader what is needed to maximize memory inside and outside the database by focusing on the following topics:

- How to determine if Oracle is being given the right amount of memory

- What new memory options in Oracle offer the most potential for improving performance

- How to keep data, code, and object definitions in memory so response times are the fastest possible

- How to quickly pinpoint user sessions that degrade response times by using excessive memory resources

Once these things are understood, the reader will be in a better position to ensure that the Oracle database is properly configured from a memory standpoint. To begin, one needs to analyze the current memory configuration and usage of the database.

Getting a Handle on Memory Usage

Not surprisingly, each release of Oracle has featured additional memory parameters that can be tweaked to create an optimal memory configuration for the database. In trained hands, these parameters can make a dramatic difference in how well the database runs. Happily, Oracle has now made these key memory settings dynamic in version 9i and above, meaning that DBAs can now size their SGA without having to start and stop the database.

The starting point with an existing database is to understand how much RAM the database server offers, and then determine the current settings of the Oracle SGA. This provides a basis for judging whether Oracle can benefit from adding or manipulating memory and how much headroom exists.

Obtaining the memory configuration of the server will depend on the hardware/operating system platform. Most operating systems have decent GUI interfaces that allow for such configuration information to be obtained through pointing and clicking. Once the memory amounts for the server are known, diagnostics should be performed to investigate the metrics of the paging/swapping situation on the server. Again, getting such information will depend on the hardware platform. However, regardless of the platform, one wants to avoid excessive paging and swapping. They tend to degrade the overall performance of anything that runs on the server since data is constantly transferred from RAM to physical swap files and then back again.

After there is a comfort level for the memory behavior on the database server, now attention will need to be turned to Oracle. The first step is to find the size of the current SGA that controls the database. To get such information, use the *sgasize.sql* script. Note that this script can be used on all Oracle versions. However, some of the columns may be *null* or zero because certain memory regions are not available in all versions.

⊟ sgasize.sql

```
select
        db_size_in_mb - db_caches db_buffers_in_mb,
        db_caches db_caches_mb,
        fixed_size_in_mb,
        lb_size_in_mb,
        sp_size_in_mb,
        lp_size_in_mb,
        jp_size_in_mb
from
(select
        round (max(a.bytes) / 1024 / 1024, 2)  db_size_in_mb
  from
        sys.v_$sgastat a
 where
        (a.name = 'db_block_buffers' or a.name = 'buffer_cache')),
(select
        nvl(round (sum (b.value) / 1024 / 1024, 2),0) db_caches
  from
        sys.v_$parameter b
 where
        b.name like '%k_cache_size'),
(select
        round (sum (b.bytes) / 1024 / 1024, 2) fixed_size_in_mb
  from
        sys.v_$sgastat b
 where
         b.name = 'fixed_sga'),
(select
        round (sum (c.bytes) / 1024 / 1024, 2) lb_size_in_mb
  from
        sys.v_$sgastat c
 where
         c.name=  'log_buffer' ),
(select
        round (sum (d.value) / 1024 / 1024, 2) sp_size_in_mb
  from
        sys.v_$parameter d
 where
         d.name = 'shared_pool_size'),
(select
        round (sum (e.value) / 1024 / 1024, 2) lp_size_in_mb
  from
        sys.v_$parameter e
 where
         e.name = 'large_pool_size' ),
(select
```

```
        round (sum (f.value) / 1024 / 1024, 2) jp_size_in_mb
  from
        sys.v_$parameter f
  where
        f.name = 'java_pool_size');
```

	DB_BUFFERS_IN_MB	DB_CACHES	FIXED_SIZE_IN_MB	LB_SIZE_IN_MB	SP_SIZE_IN_MB	LP_SIZE_IN_MB	JP_SIZE_IN_MB
1	56	16	.43	.63	48	8	32

Figure 3.11: *Getting a Summary of Oracle SGA Settings*

This script delivers more detailed information than the standard *show sga* command in the server manager or SQL*Plus because it breaks down the standard buffer cache, showing the total amount of memory given to the special 9i and above data caches and displaying information for the large and java pools.

Summary

Oracle database performance concerns in regards with database design issues are the subject of this chapter. One such feature, *autoextend*, that allows Oracle to automatically grow a datafile to meet the need of incoming or changed data if not enough free space currently exists in the tablespace was given special attention. Other performance problems regarding storage, object and database fragmentation and memory were also examined. The topic of the next chapter deals with the System Global Area and how Oracle uses it.

Oracle System Global Area

Understanding the SGA

Most DBAs know all about the Oracle System Global Area (SGA). The SGA is Oracle's structural memory area that facilitates the transfer of data and information between clients and the Oracle database. Long gone are the days when only four main tunable components existed. If one is using Oracle 9i or above, expect to deal with the following memory regions:

- *Default* buffer cache: This is the default memory cache that stores data blocks when they are read from the database. If the DBA does not specifically place objects in another data cache, then any data requested by clients from the database will be placed into this cache. This memory area is controlled by the *db_block_buffers* parameter in Oracle 8i and below, and *db_cache_size* in Oracle 9i and above.

- *Keep* buffer cache: Beginning with Oracle 8, objects can be assigned to a special cache that will retain those object's requested blocks in RAM for as long as the database is up. The *keep* cache's main function is to hold frequently referenced lookup tables that should always be kept in memory for quick access. The *buffer_pool_keep* parameter controls the size of this cache in Oracle 8, while the *db_keep_cache_size* parameter handles the cache in Oracle 9i and above. The *keep* pool is a sub-pool of the *default* buffer cache.

- *Recycle* buffer cache: Imagine the opposite of the *keep* cache, and this is the *recycle* cache. When large table scans occur, the data filling a memory cache is unlikely to be needed again and should be quickly discarded from RAM. By placing this data into the *recycle* cache, it will neither occupy valuable memory space nor prevent blocks that are needed from being placed in a buffer. However, should it be requested again, the discarded data is quickly available. The *buffer_pool_recycle* parameter controls the size of this cache in Oracle 8 and below, while the *db_recycle_cache_size* parameter handles the cache in Oracle 9i and above.

- Specific block size caches: Beginning in Oracle 9i, tablespaces can be created whose blocksize differs from the overall database blocksize. When data is read into the SGA from these tablespaces, their data has to be placed into memory regions that can accommodate their special blocksize. Oracle 9i and above has memory settings for 2K, 4K, 8K, 16K, and 32K caches. The configuration parameter names are in the pattern of *db_nk_cache_size*.

- Shared pool: This familiar area holds object structures and code definitions as well as other metadata. Setting the proper amount of memory in the shared pool assists a great deal in improving overall performance with respect to code execution and object references. The *shared_pool_size* parameter controls this memory region.

- Large pool: Starting in Oracle 8, one can configure an optional, specialized memory region called the large pool that holds items for shared server operations, backup and restore tasks, and other miscellaneous things. The *large_pool_size* parameter controls this memory region. The large pool is also used for sorting when the multi-threaded server (MTS) is implemented.

- Java pool: This area handles the memory for Java methods, class definitions and such. The *java_pool_size* parameter controls the amount of memory for this area.

- Redo log buffer: This area buffers modifications that are made to the database before they are physically written to the redo log files. The *log_buffer* configuration parameter controls this memory area.

Note that Oracle also maintains a fixed area in the SGA that contains a number of atomic variables, pointers, and other miscellaneous structures that reference areas of the SGA.

Gaining Insight into Memory Use

Once the current settings of one's SGA are understood, the next task is to see how well it is being utilized. Use a number of key ratios and wait metrics to assemble a global picture of SGA performance.

Before using the following scripts to obtain key memory metrics, be aware that some database professionals passionately believe that ratio-based analysis is a worthless endeavor and only favor a wait-based or bottleneck approach instead. There are certainly valid reasons for not relying solely on ratios to determine if the database is functioning properly.

However, when practiced correctly, ratio-based analysis is indeed worthwhile and can contribute to one's understanding of system performance. Chapter 2 about ratio-based and bottleneck analysis provides more information on this topic. That said, what are some of the key indicators of memory efficiency and usage? Rather than list each metric in a single script, the *memsnap.sql* script obtains many key memory metrics in a single query and presents them all at once.

💾 **memsnap.sql**

```
select
        buffer_hit_ratio,
        percent_shared_pool_free,
        lib_cache_hit_ratio,
        object_reloads,
        dd_cache_hit_ratio,
        redo_log_space_waits,
        redo_log_space_wait_time,
        mem_sort_ratio,
        parse_execute_ratio,
        buffer_busy_waits,
        latch_miss_ratio
from
(select
        100 -
        100 *
        (round ((sum (decode (name, 'physical reads', value, 0)) -
         sum (decode (name, 'physical reads direct', value, 0)) -
         sum (decode (name,
         'physical reads direct (lob)', value, 0))) /
         (sum (decode (name,
         'session logical reads', value, 1))),3)) buffer_hit_ratio
    from
```

```
        sys.v_$sysstat
 where
        name in ('session logical reads',
                 'physical reads direct (lob)',
                 'physical reads', 'physical reads direct')),
(select
        round (100 * (free_bytes / shared_pool_size), 2)
        percent_shared_pool_free
   from
        (select
                sum (bytes) free_bytes
          from
                sys.v_$sgastat
          where
                name = 'free memory'
            and
                pool = 'shared pool'),
        (select
                value shared_pool_size
           from
                sys.v_$parameter
           where
                name = 'shared_pool_size')),
(select
        100 - round ((sum (reloads) /
        sum (pins)) * 100, 2) lib_cache_hit_ratio
   from
        sys.v_$librarycache),
(select
        100 - round ((sum (getmisses) /
        (sum (gets) + sum (getmisses)) * 100), 2) dd_cache_hit_ratio
from    sys.v_$rowcache),
(select round (
        (100 * b.value) /
        decode ((a.value + b.value), 0, 1, (a.value + b.value)),
        2)mem_sort_ratio
   from
        v$sysstat a,
        v$sysstat b
 where
        a.name = 'sorts (disk)'
   and b.name = 'sorts (memory)'),
(select
        round(100 * (sum (sys.v_$latch.misses) /
        sum (sys.v_$latch.gets)),2) latch_miss_ratio
   from
        sys.v_$latch),
(select
        round (100 * (a.value - b.value) /
        decode (a.value, 0, 1, a.value), 2) parse_execute_ratio
   from
        sys.v_$sysstat a,
        sys.v_$sysstat b
 where
        a.name = 'execute count'
   and b.name = 'parse count (hard)'),
(select
        nvl(sum(total_waits),0) buffer_busy_waits
from
```

```
        sys.v_$system_event a,
        sys.v_$event_name b
where
        a.event = 'buffer busy waits' and
        a.event (+) = b.name),
(select
        sum(reloads) object_reloads
  from
        sys.v_$librarycache),
(select
        value redo_log_space_waits
  from
        sys.v_$sysstat
where
        name = 'redo log space requests'),
(select
        value redo_log_space_wait_time
  from
        sys.v_$sysstat
where
        name = 'redo log space wait time');
```

	BUFFER_HIT_RATIO	LIB_CACHE_HIT_RATIO	OBJECT_RELOADS	DD_CACHE_HIT_RATIO	MEM_SORT_RATIO	PARSE_EXECUTE_RATIO	PERCENT_SHARED_POOL_FREE
1	99.9	99.99	9	94.93	99.89	98.12	69.33

Figure 4.1: *Partial Output Showing Key Memory Usage Metrics*

The buffer cache hit ratio (BCHR) is the first statistic shown in the above script. As mentioned, many DBAs today maintain that this measure is not a good indicator of performance, but is this actually true?

The Buffer Cache Hit Ratio – Still Worthwhile?

The BCHR indicates how often data is found in memory vs. disk. Critics of this ratio complain that it is not a good indicator of performance because (a) many analysts use cumulative numbers for the computations, which can artificially inflate the value to a meaningless measure, and (b) it does not negatively reflect excessive logical I/O activity, which, although faster than disk I/O, can certainly suppress performance on any database.

These complaints have merit. One must use delta statistics over time to come up with a meaningful value for the ratio, and high logical I/O values can definitely be a leading cause of bad execution times. However, when properly computed, the BCHR is an excellent indicator of how often the data requested by users is found in RAM instead of disk, a fact of no small importance. The global statistic shown above is a good place to start, but one does not have to stop there. Penetrate deeper to find cache hit ratios at the buffer pool, session, and SQL statement level.

If a *keep* and *recycle* buffer pool is used in addition to the default buffer cache, utilize the *poolhit.sql* script to find the hit rates in each pool:

⊟ poolhit.sql

```
select
        name,
        100 * (1 - (physical_reads / (db_block_gets +
        consistent_gets))) hit_ratio
from
        sys.v$buffer_pool_statistics
where
        db_block_gets + consistent_gets > 0;
```

Output from the previous query might look like the following:

```
NAME        HIT_RATIO
---------- ----------
DEFAULT        92.82
KEEP           93.98
RECYCLE        85.05
```

From the overall buffer caches, turn to the cache hit ratios for user processes. The *sesshitrate.sql* script below will provide a BCHR for all currently connected sessions:

⊟ sesshitrate.sql

```
select
        b.sid sid,
        decode (b.username,null,e.name,b.username)
        user_name,
        d.spid os_id,
        b.machine machine_name,
        to_char(logon_time,'mm/dd/yy hh:mi:ss pm')
        logon_time,
        100 - 100 *
        (round ((sum (decode (c.name,
        'physical reads', value, 0)) -
        sum (decode (c.name,
        'physical reads direct', value, 0)) -
        sum(decode (c.name,
        'physical reads direct (lob)', value, 0))) /
```

```
        (sum (decode (c.name,
        'db block gets', value, 1)) +
        sum (decode (c.name,
        'consistent gets', value, 0))),3)) hit_ratio
from
        sys.v_$sesstat a,
        sys.v_$session b,
        sys.v_$statname c,
        sys.v_$process d,
        sys.v_$bgprocess e
where
        a.statistic#=c.statistic# and
        b.sid=a.sid  and
        d.addr = b.paddr and
        e.paddr (+) = b.paddr  and
        c.name in ('physical reads',
                    'physical reads direct',
                    'physical writes direct (lob)',
                    'physical reads direct (lob)',
                    'db block gets',
                    'consistent gets')
group by
        b.sid,
        d.spid,
        decode (b.username,null,e.name,b.username),
        b.machine,
        to_char(logon_time,'mm/dd/yy hh:mi:ss pm')
order by
        6 desc;
```

Query | Results

	SID	USER_NAME	OS_ID	MACHINE_NAME	LOGON_TIME	HIT_RATIO
1	1	PMON	292	EBT2K11	01/03/03 01:01:16 pm	100
2	2	DBW0	1148	EBT2K11	01/03/03 01:01:16 pm	100
3	3	LGWR	304	EBT2K11	01/03/03 01:01:16 pm	100
4	6	RECO	1136	EBT2K11	01/03/03 01:01:17 pm	100
5	8	SYS	2552	EBT2K\BILLYWS	01/17/03 02:59:01 pm	100
6	9	QVIN	2420	EBT2K\BILLYWS	01/17/03 02:39:55 pm	100
7	12	SYSMAN	2948	EBT2K\EBT2K11	01/07/03 10:29:04 am	100
8	14	SYSMAN	2800	EBT2K\EBT2K11	01/07/03 10:29:05 am	100
9	15	SYSMAN	1424	EBT2K\EBT2K11	01/07/03 10:29:05 am	100
10	24	ERADMIN	452	EBT2K\ROBINWS	01/16/03 10:27:14 am	100
11	23	USER21	3176	EBT2K\EBT2K12	01/17/03 03:59:10 pm	100
12	22	SYS	2312	EBT2K\BILLYWS	01/17/03 03:32:51 pm	100
13	21	USER21	2136	EBT2K\EBT2K12	01/14/03 11:12:56 am	100
14	19	SYSMAN	1560	EBT2K\EBT2K11	01/07/03 10:29:05 am	100
15	18	SYS	3972	EBT2K\BILLYWS	01/17/03 03:02:23 pm	100
16	17	SYSMAN	2000	EBT2K\EBT2K11	01/07/03 10:29:05 am	100
17	13	SYSMAN	236	EBT2K\EBT2K11	01/07/03 10:29:05 am	100
18	30	SYS	3752	EBT2K\ROBINWS	01/16/03 09:27:38 am	100
19	29	SYS	3620	EBT2K\BILLYWS	01/17/03 02:57:11 pm	100
20	27	SYS	1884	EBT2K\ROBINWS	01/17/03 03:55:18 pm	100
21	26	SYS	3128	EBT2K\ROBINWS	01/17/03 03:59:45 pm	100
22	11	SYSMAN	2952	EBT2K\EBT2K11	01/07/03 10:29:04 am	100
23	4	CKPT	1176	EBT2K11	01/03/03 01:01:17 pm	100
24	5	SMON	1236	EBT2K11	01/03/03 01:01:17 pm	99.8
25	25	SYSTEM	612	EBT2K\EBT2K11	01/07/03 10:29:44 am	99.5

Figure 4.2: *Sample Output Showing Session Hit Ratio Information*

After examining the session hit ratio information, move into SQL statement analysis with the *sqlhitrate.sql* script:

sqlhitrate.sql

```
select
        sql_text ,
        b.username ,
        100 - round(100 *
        a.disk_reads/greatest(a.buffer_gets,1),2) hit_ratio
from
        sys.v_$sqlarea a,
        sys.all_users b
```

```
where
        a.parsing_user_id=b.user_id and
        b.username not in ('SYS','SYSTEM')
order by
        3 desc;
```

	SQL_TEXT	USERNAME	HIT_RATIO
1	SELECT 1035, COUNT(*) FROM SYS.SEG$ S,SYS.TS$ TS WHERE S.TS# = TS.TS# AND DECODE(BITAND(TS.FLAGS, 3), 1, TO_NUMBER(NULL),S.EXTSIZE	USER1	100
2	COMMIT	QVIN	100
3	SELECT 980, CHAINEDFETCHES,TOTALFETCHES FROM (SELECT VALUE AS CHAINEDFETCHES FROM SYS.V_$SYSSTAT A WHERE NAME='table fetch	USER1	100
4	SELECT 1036, COUNT(*) FROM (SELECT ROUND((100*Sum_Free_Blocks / Sum_Alloc_Blocks),2) PCT_FREE FROM (SELECT Tablespace_Name,SUM(Blocks) Sum_Alloc_Blocks,SUM(bytes) AS Total_space FROM SYS.DBA_DATA_FILES GROUP BY Tablespace_Name), (SELECT	USER1	100
5	SELECT /*+ ALL_ROWS IGNORE_WHERE_CLAUSE */ NVL(SUM(C1),0), NVL(SUM(C2),0), COUNT(DISTINCT C3) FROM (SELECT /*+	QVIN	100
6	COMMIT WORK	QVIN	100
7	/* OracleOEM */ UPDATE smp_vdp_node_info SET status = 'N', DOWN_TIME = :1, DOWN_TIMEZONE = :2 WHERE (status = 'Y') AND (node = :3) AND	SYSMAN	100
8	begin PERFCNTR_DRILLDOWN_QUERIES.fetchcursor_10(QUERY_LIST_IN=>'914',MAX _ROWS_IN=>500,VAR1_OUT=>:R001C001,VAR2_OUT=>:R001C002,VAR3_OU	USER1	100
9	SELECT 976, ROUND(A.VALUE/1048576,2) DB,ROUND(B.VALUE/1048576,2) FS,ROUND(C.VALUE/1048576,2) RB,ROUND(D.VALUE/1048576,2) VS FROM	USER1	100
10	LOCK TABLE smp_vdp_node_oms_map IN EXCLUSIVE MODE	SYSMAN	100
11	LOCK TABLE smp_vdg_gateway_map in EXCLUSIVE MODE	SYSMAN	100
12	SELECT 1033, b.USERNAME,b.SID,b.SERIAL#,B.STATUS,DECODE((SUBSTR(B.MACHINE,LENG TH(B.MACHINE),1)),CHR(0),(SUBSTR(B.MACHINE,1,LENGTH(B.MACHINE)-1)),RT RIM(B.MACHINE)) MACHINE,ROUND(SUM(DECODE(c.NAME,'session pga memory',VALUE,0))/1024,2) pga_memory,ROUND(SUM(DECODE(c.NAME,'session uga memory',VALUE,0))/1024,2) uga_memory,ROUND(SUM(DECODE(c.NAME, 'sorts	USER1	100

Figure 4.3: *Sample Output Showing SQL Statement Hit Ratio Analysis*

One nuance in the SQL hit ratio script, as well as the buffer pool script which calculates hit rates for the different buffer pools, that one should be aware of is that the Oracle *v$sqlarea* view does not provide a way to filter direct reads, i.e. physical reads that do not pass through the buffer cache, and consequently do not increment any logical I/O counters. This means it is possible to have a SQL statement that prompts a lot of direct reads, while the hit ratio shows negative.

Exploiting Non-standard Data Caches

In Oracle 9i and above, tablespaces can be created with blocksizes that differ from the overall database blocksize. If one chooses to do this, then one must also enable one or more of the new *db_nk_cache_size* parameters so that blocks read in from tablespaces that have a different blocksize than the regular database blocksize have a cache to reside in. For example, if a tablespace is created with a 16K blocksize, then one must also set aside RAM for those blocks using the *db_16k_cache_size* parameter. Note that such allocations are in addition to the memory allotments specified by the *db_cache_size* parameter.

This feature allows a DBA to tune her database in ways that were impossible in earlier versions of Oracle. For example, use the large (16-32K) blocksize data caches to store data from indexes or tables that are the object of repeated large scans. Does such a thing really help performance? A small but revealing test can answer that question.

For the test, the following query will be used against a 9i database that has a database block size of 8K, but also has the 16K cache enabled along with a 16K tablespace:

```
select
      count(*)
from
      eradmin.admission
where
      patient_id between 1 and 40000;
```

The *eradmin.admission* table has 150,000 rows in it and has an index build on the *patient_id* column. An *explain* of the query reveals that it uses an index range scan to produce the desired end result:

```
Execution Plan
-----------------------------------------------------------
SELECT STATEMENT Optimizer=CHOOSE
(Cost=41 Card=1 Bytes=4)
   1    0   SORT (AGGREGATE)
   2    1     INDEX (FAST FULL SCAN) OF 'admission_patientT_id'
              (NON-UNIQUE) (Cost=41 Card=120002 Bytes=480008)
```

Executing the query twice to eliminate parse activity and to cache any data with the index residing in a standard 8K tablespace produces these runtime statistics:

```
Statistics
---------------------------------------------------
          0   recursive calls
          0   db block gets
        421   consistent gets
          0   physical reads
          0   redo size
        371   bytes sent via SQL*Net to client
        430   bytes received via SQL*Net from client
          2   SQL*Net roundtrips to/from client
          0   sorts (memory)
          0   sorts (disk)
          1   rows processed
```

To test the effectiveness of the new 16K cache and 16K tablespace, the index used by the query will be rebuilt into the larger tablespace, while everything else remains the same:

```
alter index
      eradmin.admission_patient_id
      rebuild nologging noreverse tablespace indx_16k;
```

Once the index is nestled firmly into the 16K tablespace, the query is re-executed (again, twice) with the following runtime statistics being produced:

```
Statistics
---------------------------------------------------
          0   recursive calls
          0   db block gets
        211   consistent gets
          0   physical reads
          0   redo size
        371   bytes sent via SQL*Net to client
        430   bytes received via SQL*Net from client
          2   SQL*Net roundtrips to/from client
          0   sorts (memory)
          0   sorts (disk)
          1   rows processed
```

As one can see, the amount of logical reads has been cut in half simply by using the new 16K tablespace and accompanying 16K data cache. Clearly, the benefits of the proper use of the new data caches and multiblock tablespace features of Oracle 9i are worth investigating and testing in one's own database.

Other Interesting Buffer Cache Metrics

If a deeper understanding of how the buffer cache is being utilized is desired, there are a few additional queries that can be run to gain such insight. If the *keep* and *recycle* buffer caches are being used, run the *cacheobjcnt.sql* query to get an idea on how many objects have been assigned to each cache:

🖫 cacheobjcnt.sql

```
select
      decode(cachehint, 0, 'default', 1,
      'keep', 2, 'recycle', null) cache,
      count(*) objects
from
      sys.seg$ s
where
      s.user#  in
      (select
          user#
       from
          sys.user$
       where
          name not in ('sys','system'))
group by
      decode(cachehint, 0, 'default', 1,
      'keep', 2, 'recycle', null)
order by
    1;
```

Output may resemble something like the following:

```
CACHE       OBJECTS
----------------
default        2023
keep              5
```

Finally, one may wish to analyze the buffer cache activity from time to time to see how it is being utilized. The *buffutl.sql* script will show how full the cache currently is along with the state of the buffers in the cache:

🖫 buffutl.sql

```
select
      'free' buffer_state,
```

```
        nvl(sum(blocksize) / 1024 ,0) amt_kb
from
        sys.x$bh a,
        sys.ts$ b
where
        state = 0  and
        a.ts#  =  b.ts#
union all
select
        'read/mod' buffer_state,
        nvl(sum(blocksize) / 1024 ,0) amt_kb
from
        sys.x$bh a,
        sys.ts$ b
where
        state = 1  and
        a.ts#  =  b.ts#
union all
select
        'read/notmod',
        nvl(sum(blocksize) / 1024 ,0) amt_kb
from
        sys.x$bh a,
        sys.ts$ b
where
        state = 2  and
        a.ts#  =  b.ts#
union all
select
        'being read' buffer_state,
        nvl(sum(blocksize) / 1024 ,0) amt_kb
from
        sys.x$bh a,
        sys.ts$ b
where
        state = 3  and
        a.ts#  =  b.ts#
order by
        1;
```

Output from the above query might look something like this:

```
BUFFER_STATE        AMT_KB
----------------------
being read            5920
free                 23568
read/mod             47952
read/notmod              0
```

Summary

Oracle's System Global Area (SGA), which is the structural memory area that facilitates the transfer of data and information between clients and the Oracle database, was the topic of this chapter. Memory regions such as the default, keep and recycle buffer caches were examined. The Buffer Cache Hit Ratio (BCHR), which was introduced in Chapter 2, was given more attention. Also, several scripts involving memory regions were given as examples to help the reader better understand this important component of Oracle databases.

Hopefully this has given the DBA a good understanding of how to interrogate the buffer cache, so now the next area to be examined is the shared pool.

The Shared Pool and I/O Troubleshooting

Troubleshooting the Shared Pool

The four metrics below are revealed by the *memsnap.sql* query, after the buffer cache hit ratio (BCHR), and concern the shared pool. Execution response times can be adversely affected if Oracle has to handle parse activity, perform object definition lookups, or manage other code-related or reference tasks.

The shared pool helps Oracle keep these reference-related activities to a minimum by holding SQL statements, along with code and object definitions, in memory. As with the data cache, properly sizing the shared pool can be tricky and often involves trial and error. The *memsnap.sql* query reveals that a shared pool that is sized too small has the following characteristics:

- Zero or near-zero percent free in the pool after the database has only been up a short while

- A library cache hit ratio that is below average (95% or below)

- Many object reloads due to definitions being forced from the pool prematurely

- A below average data dictionary cache hit ratio (95% or below)

The last three metrics mentioned above should be viewed in the same light as the BCHR in that delta measurements often produce more meaningful results than cumulative measurements, and some databases will perform quite well with measures that appear non-optimal.

With respect to the percent free in the shared pool, a near zero reading after the database has been up for some time is probably fine. But if the pool drops to zero free shortly after Oracle is started, that is a strong indication that it may be sized too small.

When Does Less Become More?

So, why not just size the shared pool to some huge number and be done? First, as with sizing the data cache, an eye should be kept on available memory at the server level so that paging or swapping is not induced when RAM is added to the shared pool.

However, the main reason to not oversize the shared pool is that sometimes a large pool actually causes reduced response times. How can this happen? The simple explanation is that it takes Oracle longer to search for object definitions or SQL statements in a shared pool that is gargantuan. Oracle will always try and reuse SQL statements to keep from re-parsing a query, and while this can certainly reduce execution times when a shared pool is sized correctly, it can actually hinder progress when the pool is so large that Oracle wastes time interrogating it.

Viewing Shared Pool Usage Internals

While the global ratios and metrics can provide a rough idea of how efficient the shared pool is, looking deeper will provide more details on how the pool is being utilized and whether it is sized correctly.

The two main areas of the shared pool are the library and data dictionary caches. The library cache holds commonly used SQL statements, basically database code objects. One excellent method of improving performance in Oracle is to encourage the reuse of SQL statements so that expensive parse operations are avoided. The library cache assists this tuning effort.

The data dictionary cache enables the sharing of object definition information. The dictionary cache stores the description of database structures so that needed structure references can be resolved as quickly as possible. There are three queries that can be used to extract the details of library cache usage. The *libdet.sql* script will show which object types are taking longer to find than others:

💾 **libdet.sql**

```
select
        namespace,
        gets,
        round(gethitratio*100,2) gethitratio,
        pins,
        round(pinhitratio*100,2) pinhitratio,
        reloads,
        invalidations
from
        sys.v_$librarycache
order by
        1;
```

	NAMESPACE	GETS	GETHITRATIO	PINS	PINHITRATIO	RELOADS	INVALIDATIONS
1	BODY	7755	99.47	7761	99.34	0	0
2	CLUSTER	9962	99.84	6838	99.62	0	0
3	INDEX	682	54.99	408	20.34	0	0
4	JAVA DATA	16	62.5	61	73.77	2	0
5	JAVA RESOURCE	0	100	0	100	0	0
6	JAVA SOURCE	16	81.25	22	50	2	0
7	OBJECT	0	100	0	100	0	0
8	PIPE	0	100	0	100	0	0
9	SQL AREA	2491828	99.56	11586427	99.8	1039	5494
10	TABLE/PROCEDURE	499978	99	3052161	99.64	1338	0
11	TRIGGER	44032	99.92	44039	99.91	0	0

Figure 5.1: *Extracting the Library Cache Details*

Bottleneck or wait-based analysis can be used in addition to ratios and drill down queries to get an idea of overall library cache health. The *libwait.sql* query provides clues about whether Oracle has been waiting for library cache activities:

💾 **libwait.sql**

```
select
      b.name,
      nvl(max(a.total_waits),0)
from
```

```
        sys.v_$system_event a,
        sys.v_$event_name b
where
        a.event (+)  = b.name and
        b.name in ('latch free','library cache load lock',
                   'library cache lock','library cache pin')
group by
        b.name
```

Output from the above script might resemble the following:

```
NAME                        WAITS
-------------------------------
latch free                    16
library cache load lock        2
library cache lock             0
library cache pin              0
```

Seeing increasing numbers of waits for the above events could indicate an undersized shared pool. Dig even deeper into the library cache and uncover exactly which objects currently reside in the cache.

The *libobj.sql* script will show everything a DBA needs to know on this front, but be forewarned as this script can return large amounts of data in databases with large shared pools and many references to code and data objects:

🖫 **libobj.sql**

```
select
        owner,
        name,
        type,
        sharable_mem,
        loads,
        executions,
        locks,
        pins,
        kept
from
        sys.v_$db_object_cache
order by
        type asc;
```

	OWNER	NAME	TYPE	SHARABLE_MEM	LOADS
8	[NULL]	select i.obj#, i.flags, u.name, o.name from sys.obj$ o, sys.user$ u, ind$ idx, sys.indpart$ i	CURSOR	11416	1
9	[NULL]	select /*+ rule */ bucket_cnt, row_cnt, cache_cnt, null_cnt, timestamp#, sample_size, minimum,	CURSOR	10468	1
10	[NULL]	select i.obj#, i.flags, u.name, o.name from sys.obj$ o, sys.user$ u, ind$ idx, sys.indpart$ i	CURSOR	1064	1
11	[NULL]	select /*+ rule */ bucket_cnt, row_cnt, cache_cnt, null_cnt, timestamp#, sample_size, minimum,	CURSOR	1068	1
12	[NULL]	select grantee#,privilege#,nvl(col#,0),max(nvl(opti	CURSOR	1003	1
13	[NULL]	SELECT 1 FROM SYS.OBJ$ WHERE OWNER# =1	CURSOR	920	1
14	[NULL]	select privilege#,nvl(col#,0),max(nvl(option$,0))fro	CURSOR	982	1
15	[NULL]	select signature from triggerjavas$ where obj#=:1	CURSOR	4224	1
16	[NULL]	select class_name, class_factory, class_factory_	CURSOR	966	1
17	[NULL]	select class_name, class_factory, class_factory_	CURSOR	5516	1
18	[NULL]	select flags from triggerjavaf$ where obj#=:1	CURSOR	903	1
19	[NULL]	select flags from triggerjavaf$ where obj#=:1	CURSOR	4524	1
20	[NULL]	select text from view$ where rowid=:1	CURSOR	895	1
21	[NULL]	select text from view$ where rowid=:1	CURSOR	4252	1
22	[NULL]	select privilege#,nvl(col#,0),max(nvl(option$,0))fro	CURSOR	6848	1
23	[NULL]	SELECT 1 FROM SYS.OBJ$ WHERE OWNER# =1	CURSOR	6960	1
24	[NULL]	insert into uet$ (segfile#,segblock#,ext#,ts#,file#,b	CURSOR	5756	1
25	[NULL]	select count (*), state from SYSTEM.DEF$_AQER	CURSOR	940	1

Figure 5.2: *Drilling Down into the Library Cache*

Using the above script, it can be seen how often an object has been loaded into the cache. Many loads could indicate that the object is continuously being forced from the cache, which would potentially degrade performance. If the object is a code object such as a procedure or package, pin the code in the cache to stop it from being removed. In the above query, reference the kept column to see which code objects, if any, have already been pinned.

The *dbms_shared_pool* package is used to pin or unpin code objects to and from the library cache. For example, if there is a frequently referenced procedure called *eradmin.add_admission* and wanted to make sure that it would always be found in the library cache for quick reference, then execute the following:

```
exec sys.dbms_shared_pool.keep('ERADMIN.ADD_ADMISSION','P');
```

Performing a pin keeps the code where it should be at all times. Pinned objects are also impervious to an *alter system flush shared_pool* command. While this technique works well for code objects, what about regular SQL statements? How can they be kept in the shared pool so that parse operations are minimized? The easiest method is to ensure that user sessions are launching identical SQL statements, which allows reuse to occur in the cache.

If Oracle detects that a user process has launched an identical SQL statement that is already present in the cache, it will reuse the statement rather than parse and load it into memory. Using literals in SQL statements instead of bind variables can greatly hinder this process from occurring. Again, the key to statement reuse is that the SQL has to be identical, and the use of literals in SQL statements can entirely negate this.

If a DBA is not able to encase the user's SQL in applications or stored code objects to ensure bind variables are being used instead of literals, what should be done? In version 8.1.6, Oracle quietly introduced the *cursor_sharing* parameter, which can deal with the problem of literals in otherwise identical SQL statements in a hurry.

If this parameter is set to *force*, Oracle will substitute bind variables in the place of literals in any SQL statement and place it into the library cache. This permits any statement submitted subsequently to be reused, so long as the only difference is its bind variable(s).

Is there anything else that should be looked into with respect to the shared pool? One other area of interest is the data dictionary cache.

More Shared Pool Metrics

To see how often Oracle is finding the system references it needs in the data dictionary, use the *dictdet.sql* script which is sorted from best-hit ratio to worst:

🖫 dictdet.sql

```
select
        parameter,
        usage,
        gets,
        getmisses,
        100 - round((getmisses/
        (gets + getmisses) * 100),2) hit_ratio
from
        sys.v_$rowcache
where
        gets + getmisses <> 0
order by
        5 desc;
```

	PARAMETER	USAGE	GETS	GETMISSES	HIT_RATIO
1	dc_profiles	1	37318	1	100
2	dc_tablespaces	20	287977	20	99.99
3	dc_users	39	393939	42	99.99
4	dc_rollback_segments	12	106272	11	99.99
5	dc_user_grants	36	172771	48	99.97
6	dc_files	14	35355	14	99.96
7	dc_usernames	18	94137	35	99.96
8	dc_sequences	5	3426	18	99.48
9	dc_global_oids	19	1477	19	98.73
10	dc_tablespace_quotas	14	974	16	98.38
11	dc_object_ids	1037	82692	1521	98.19
12	dc_segments	629	41262	916	97.83
13	dc_objects	1638	77893	4367	94.69
14	dc_histogram_defs	1262	19592	2241	89.74
15	dc_constraints	1	1482	748	66.46
16	dc_table_scns	0	6	6	50

Figure 5.3: *Drilling Down into the Dictionary Cache*

Just as with the library cache, a high data dictionary cache hit ratio is desirable. It is optimal to strive for a hit ratio between 90 - 100%, with 95% being a good rule-of-thumb benchmark.

Note that when a database is first started, the overall data dictionary cache hit ratio as well as the individual hit ratios in the above query will not be at an optimal level. This is because all references to object definitions will be relatively new, and as such, must be placed into the shared pool. Look for hit ratios between eighty and ninety percent for new database startups. If, however, after a solid hour or two of steady database time, the data dictionary cache hit ratio has not increased to desirable levels, look into the possibility of increasing the *shared_pool_size* parameter.

While there is certainly more that can be explained regarding shared pools, the areas covered above are the normal hot spots. Are there any other SGA issues that should be checked periodically? One area is the redo log buffer.

Troubleshooting the Log Buffer

Sometimes a user process must wait for space in the redo log buffer. Oracle uses the log buffer to cache redo entries prior to writing them to disk, and if the buffer area is not large enough for the redo entry load, waits can occur. The log buffer is normally small in comparison with other regions of the SGA, and a small increase in size can significantly enhance throughput.

In high-update databases, no amount of disk tuning may relieve redo log bottlenecks because Oracle must push all updates, for all disks, into a single redo location (Figure 5.4):

Redo is a natural bottleneck for high-update databases because
Oracle redo disk must accept the sum of all disk update rates.

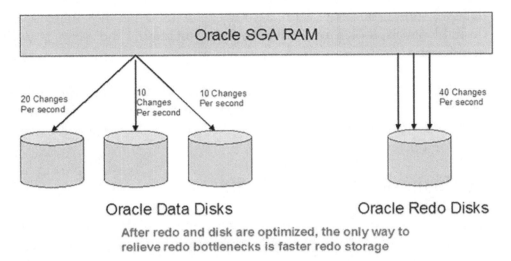

Figure 5.4: *Oracle Redo Bottleneck*

The *memsnap.sql* script contains two main numbers to watch for in the log buffer, which are:

- Rredo log space requests
- Redo log wait time

If either statistic strays too far from 0, then it may be possible to increase the *log_buffer* parameter and add more memory to the redo log buffer.

The *log_buffer* is one of the most complex of the Oracle RAM region parameters to optimize, but it is a low-resource parameter, only using a few meg of RAM, so the goal in sizing *log_buffer* is to set a value that results in the least overall amount of log-related wait events. The big issue with the log buffer is determining the optimal sizing for the *log_buffer* in a busy, high-DML database. Common wait events related to a too-small *log_buffer* size include high *redo log space requests* and a too-large *log_buffer* may result in high *log file sync* waits.

Here is an AWR report showing a database with an undersized *log_buffer*, in this case where the DBA did not set the *log_buffer* parameter in their *init.ora* file:

```
                                            Avg
                                     Total Wait    wait    Waits
Event                Waits  Timeouts  Time (s)    (ms)     /txn
-------------------- ------ -------- ---------- ------   --------
log file sequential read  4,275        0        229       54      0.0
log buffer space            12        0          3      235      0.0


Top 5 Timed Events
~~~~~~~~~~~~~~~~~~~
                                                         % Total
Event                              Waits      Time (s)  Ela Time
---------------------------------- ---------- --------- --------
CPU time                                        163,182   88.23
db file sequential read            1,541,854     8,551    4.62
log file sync                      1,824,469     8,402    4.54
log file parallel write            1,810,628     2,413    1.30
SQL*Net more data to client       15,421,202       687     .37
```

It is important to note that log buffer shortages do not always manifest in the top 5 timed events, especially if there are other SGA pool shortages. Here is an example of an Oracle 10g database with an undersized log buffer; in this example, 512k where there was a serious data buffer shortage causing excessive disk I/O:

```
Top 5 Timed Events
~~~~~~~~~~~~~~~~~~~
                                                  % Total
Event                      Waits   Time (s)   DB Time   Wait Class
-------------------------- ------  --------- --------- ----------
log file parallel write     9,670      291    55.67    System I/O
log file sync               9,293      278    53.12    Commit
CPU time                               225    43.12
db file parallel write      4,922      201    38.53    System I/O
control file parallel write 1,282       65    12.42    System I/O
```

Log Buffer Related Parameter Issues

In addition to resizing *log_buffer*, the hidden Oracle10g parameter *_log_io_size* can also be adjusted, but only at the direction of Oracle technical support, and then the *transactions_per_rollback_segment* parameters are adjusted. In 10g, the *_log_io_size* parameter governs the offload threshold and it defaults to *log_buffer/3*. The *transactions_per_rollback_segment* parameter specifies the number of concurrent transactions one expects each rollback segment to have to handle.

Today, most large databases use a log buffer between 5 meg to 10 meg. It is important to note that log buffer shortages do not always manifest in the top 5 timed events, especially if there are other SGA pool shortages, and remember that the optimal *log_buffer* size is a function of the commit rate and redo log volume.

Once the DBA has a handle on how the SGA is performing globally, they might want to look into memory usage at the session level to see which processes are consuming the most resources and making life miserable for everyone.

Investigating Session Memory Usage

Even though Oracle has built-in governors, it is not uncommon for one or two users to cause runtime problems that plague an entire database. The problem could be a runaway process, an un-tuned batch procedure, or other user-initiated operations. Sometimes user connection memory consumption can get out of hand, and extreme cases can cause headaches at both the database and operating system level, causing ORA-4030 errors. If the database server does not have an overabundance of memory, then periodically check to see who the heavy memory users are, along with the total percentage of memory each user consumes.

If there are one or two users who have more than 15-50% of the total memory usage, then the DBA should investigate the sessions further to see the kind of activities they are performing. Use the *memhog.sql* script to find the sessions that use the most memory in a database:

🖫 **memhog.sql**

```
select
       sid,
       username,
       round(total_user_mem/1024,2) mem_used_in_kb,
       round(100 * total_user_mem/total_mem,2) mem_percent
from
(select
    b.sid sid,
    nvl(b.username,p.name) username,
    sum(value) total_user_mem
from
    sys.v_$statname c,
    sys.v_$sesstat a,
    sys.v_$session b,
```

```
      sys.v_$bgprocess p
where
      a.statistic#=c.statistic# and
      p.paddr (+) = b.paddr and
      b.sid=a.sid and
      c.name in ('session pga memory','session uga memory')
group by
      b.sid, nvl(b.username,p.name)),
(select
      sum(value) total_mem
from
      sys.v_$statname c,
      sys.v_$sesstat a
where
      a.statistic#=c.statistic#
and
      c.name in ('session pga memory','session uga memory'))
order by
      3 desc;
```

	SID	USERNAME	MEM_USED_IN_KB	MEM_PERCENT
1	2	DBW0	740.92	18.28
2	14	SYS	685.63	16.91
3	7	SNP0	417.76	10.31
4	3	LGWR	295.21	7.28
5	5	SMON	275.42	6.79
6	13	SYS	232.14	5.73
7	8	SNP1	217.38	5.36
8	11	SNP4	216.77	5.35
9	9	SNP2	200.73	4.95
10	10	SNP3	200.73	4.95
11	12	DBSNMP	188.45	4.65
12	4	CKPT	172.29	4.25
13	6	RECO	150.95	3.72
14	22	SYS	86.88	2.14
15	1	PMON	76.39	1.88

Figure 5.5: *Sample Output Showing the Top Memory Users in a Database*

Another metric shown in the *memsnap.sql* script is the parse to execute ratio. It shows the percentage of SQL executed that did not incur a hard parse. Seeing low values might indicate that users are executing SQL with many hard-coded literals instead of bind variables within the application. High values (90% +) generally indicate Oracle is saving precious CPU resources by avoiding heavy parse tasks.

While the above figures help one get a handle on session memory usage within Oracle's Program Global Area (PGA) and User Global Area (UGA), another area that should be checked into is sort activity.

Investigating Sorts

The SGA is not the only memory structure used by Oracle for database work. One of the other memory regions used by Oracle 8i and below for normal activity is an area set aside for sort actions. When a sort operation occurs, Oracle attempts to perform the sort in a memory space that exists at the operating system level. If the sort is too large to be contained within this space, it will continue the sort on disk; specifically, in the user's assigned temporary tablespace.

Techniques to include in the overall performance strategy are those that relate to minimizing the amount of overall sort activity, and especially sort activity that takes place on disk. A good place to start is to understand what things cause sorts in the first place. A list of sort-related commands and SQL-related options include:

- *create index, later index...rebuild*
- *distinct*
- *order by*
- *group by*
- *union*
- *intersect*
- *minus*
- *in, not in*
- Certain unindexed joins
- Certain correlated subqueries

All of these SQL commands have the potential to create a sort. A DBA will probably not know which queries will sort entirely in memory and which ones will be forced to go to disk. However, they can get a feel for the overall sort performance by looking at the memory sort ratio that is contained in the output from the *memsnap.sql* query.

As has already been mentioned, when a sort exhausts its memory allotment, it will then be forced to go to disk, the actual place being the user's temporary tablespace assignment. Oracle records the overall number of sorts that are satisfied in memory, as well as those that end up being finalized on disk. Using these numbers, calculate the percentage of memory sorts vs. disk sorts and get a feel for how fast the sort activity is being resolved.

If the memory sort ratio falls below 90%, increasing the parameters devoted to memory sorts, *sort_area_size* and *sort_area_retained_size*, may be desired. Keep in mind that individual users may possess the ability to alter their own sessions and increase their *sort_area_size* assignments. As a DBA, it may be desirable to restrict users that have the *alter session* privilege so that this does not occur.

Troubleshooting Oracle Sorting

As has been noted, a serious problem in Oracle 8i was the requirement that all dedicated connections use a one-size-fits-all *sort_area_size*. Oracle 9i has the option of running automatic PGA memory management.

Oracle has introduced a new Oracle parameter called *pga_aggregate_target*. When the *pga_aggregate_target* parameter is set and dedicated Oracle connections are being used, Oracle 9i will ignore all of the PGA parameters in the Oracle file, including *sort_area_size*, *hash_area_size* and *sort_area_retained_size*. Oracle recommends that the value of *pga_aggregate_target* be set to the amount of remaining memory, less a 10 % overhead for other UNIX tasks, on the UNIX server after the instance has been started.

Once the *pga_aggregate_target* has been set, Oracle will automatically manage PGA memory allocation based upon the individual needs of each Oracle connection. Oracle 9i allows the *pga_aggregate_target* parameter to be modified at the instance level with the *alter system* command, thereby allowing the DBA to dynamically adjust the total RAM region available to Oracle.

Oracle 9i also introduces a new parameter called *workarea_size_policy*. When this parameter is set to automatic, all Oracle connections will benefit from the shared PGA memory. When *workarea_size_policy* is set to manual, connections will allocate memory according to the values for the *sort_area_size* parameter. Under the automatic mode, Oracle tries to maximize the number of work areas that are using optimal memory and uses one-pass memory for the others.

In addition to increasing the amount of memory devoted to sorting, it is also good to hunt down inefficient SQL that cause needless sorts. For example, *union all* does not cause a sort, whereas *union* does in a SQL query to eliminate duplicate rows. The DISTINCT keyword is oftentimes coded inappropriately, especially by folks transferring from Microsoft Access, which used to use DISTINCT for nearly every query.

The two final metrics shown in the *memsnap.sql* script deal with buffer busy waits and the latch miss ratio.

Buffer Busy Waits

Buffer busy waits occur when a process needs to access a data block in the buffer cache but cannot because it is being used by another process. So it must wait. Buffer busy waits normally center around contention for rollback segments, too small an INITRANS setting for tables, or insufficient *freelists* for tables.

The remedy for each situation would be to increase the number of rollback segments, or to alter tables for larger INITRANS settings to allow for more transactions per data block and more *freelists*. Note that the automatic segment management feature in Oracle 9i's locally-managed tablespaces can make the *freelist* problem a thing of the past, while the UNDO tablespace feature of 9i can help remedy any rollback contention problem.

However, segment header contention will still occur when concurrent tasks attempt to insert into the same table, and multiple *freelists* are required to remove these sources of buffer busy waits. If a DBA is using Oracle 9i and above, use this script to see what objects have been the sources of buffer busy waits. The *bufobjwaits.sql* script will tell everything that needs to be known:

💾 bufobjwaits.sql

```
select
      owner,
      object_name,
      object_type,
      value waits
from
      sys.v_$segment_statistics
where
      (statistic_name = 'buffer busy waits' and value > 0)
order by
      1,2;
```

OWNER	OBJECT_NAME	OBJECT_TYPE	WAITS
USR1	TAB1	TABLE	3
USR1	TAB2	TABLE	2
USR1	TAB3	TABLE	2

Troubleshooting Latches

There have been volumes written about Oracle latches. However, in case it is not known what they are, latches protect the many memory structures in Oracle's SGA. They ensure that one and only one process at a time can run or modify any memory structure at the same instant. Much more restrictive than locks, which at least allow for some collective user interaction, latches have no queuing mechanism, so if it is not gotten the first time, one is forced to continually retry.

Common indicators of latch contention are a latch miss ratio, which records willing-to-wait mode latch requests, and latch immediate miss ratio, which records no-wait mode latch requests.

These statistics reflect how often latch requests were made and satisfied without waiting. If either of these exceeds 1%, then drill down further into latching details to identify what latches are responsible for the contention.

To drill down into latch miss details, use the *latchdet.sql* script:

🖫 latchdet.sql

```
select
        name,
        gets,
        round(misses*100/decode(gets,0,1,gets),2) misses,
        round(spin_gets*100/decode(misses,0,1,misses),2) spins,
        immediate_gets igets,
        round(immediate_misses*100/
        decode(immediate_gets,0,1,immediate_gets),2) imisses,
        sleeps
from
        sys.v_$latch
order by
        2 desc;
```

	NAME	GETS	MISSES	SPINS	IGETS	IMISSES	SLEEPS
1	cache buffers chains	44409592	0	0	4724	0	30
2	cache buffers lru chain	2374631	0	0	0	0	0
3	library cache	572680	.01	0	306	0	155
4	row cache objects	399355	0	0	155	0	52
5	session idle bit	198677	0	0	0	0	0
6	shared pool	164652	0	0	0	0	1
7	enqueues	149031	0	0	0	0	0
8	messages	134876	0	0	0	0	0
9	checkpoint queue latch	82846	0	0	0	0	0
10	redo writing	82507	0	0	0	0	7
11	session allocation	66204	0	0	0	0	0
12	enqueue hash chains	63572	0	0	0	0	0
13	undo global data	29407	0	0	0	0	0
14	redo allocation	23957	.01	0	0	0	8
15	active checkpoint queue latch	20344	0	0	0	0	0
16	session timer	20297	0	0	0	0	0
17	sort extent pool	8813	0	0	0	0	0
18	JOX SGA heap latch	3720	0	0	3120	0	0
19	virtual circuit queues	3046	0	0	0	0	0
20	library cache load lock	2526	0	0	0	0	0
21	cache buffer handles	2453	.08	0	0	0	2
22	shared java pool	2289	0	0	0	0	0
23	transaction allocation	1991	.1	0	0	0	2
24	dml lock allocation	1252	0	0	0	0	0
25	longop free list	998	0	0	0	0	0
26	session switching	983	0	0	0	0	0
27	transaction branch allocation	976	0	0	0	0	0

Figure 5.6: *Output Showing Latch Details*

If the choice is to see whether any sessions are currently waiting for latches, use the *currlwaits.sql* script:

currlwaits.sql

```
select
      a.sid,
      username,
      a.event,
      p1text,
      p1,
      p2text,
      p2,
```

```
        seq#,
        wait_time,
        state
from
        sys.v_$session_wait a,
        sys.v_$session b,
        sys.v_$latchname c
where
        a.sid = b.sid and
        a.p2 = c.latch# and
        a.event in
        (select
                name
          from
            sys.v_$event_name
   where
            name like '%latch%')
order by
            1;
```

Keep in mind that catching an actual session latch wait is a difficult thing to do since they rarely consume much time.

Troubleshooting I/O Hotspots

When complaints begin to surface about the database's performance, oftentimes the root cause can be traced to one or more issues with I/O. The one thing to keep in mind when monitoring of the I/O of the database begins is that the success of the physical design model is what is really being reviewed.

All the physical storage characteristics and placements, the table and index designs, and the speed with which it all works are on display when I/O is monitored. Because a database's main index of performance is measured by how fast I/O needs are satisfied, it is the DBA's responsibility to quickly interrogate Oracle to determine if a reported database slowdown is I/O related.

How can such a task be quickly accomplished? While it is true that every situation is different in some regard, one roadmap one can regularly use is the following:

- Obtain global measures regarding the I/O of the database and note any standout values.

- Examine global statistics regarding how database objects are being accessed.

- Move deeper by examining the I/O of the storage structures and noting where the hotspots appear to be on the disk.

- From storage, uncover what objects appear to be the most in demand.

- If the reported slowdown is currently active, obtain metrics regarding the leading sessions with respect to I/O.

Once the objects and users that are responsible for the most I/O issues are known, drill further into the situation by locating the SQL being issued. Next, walk through each of these steps in detail and see how they can quickly pinpoint the I/O hotspots and bottlenecks in the database.

Global Basic Queries

The first step in unraveling any I/O puzzles in the database is to make a quick check of some of the global database I/O metrics. A query such as the *globiostats.sql* script can be used to get a bird's eye view of a database's I/O:

🖫 **globiostats.sql**

```
select
   name,
   value
from
   sys.v_$sysstat
where
   name in
    ('consistent changes',
     'consistent gets',
     'db block changes',
     'db block gets',
     'physical reads',
     'physical writes',
     'sorts (disk)',
     'user commits',
     'user rollbacks'
    )
 order by
1;
```

Output from the above query might look like the following:

```
NAME                   VALUE
-----------------------------
consistent changes         1
consistent gets        70983
db block changes         243
db block gets            612
physical reads         11591
physical writes           52
sorts (disk)               0
user commits              26
user rollbacks             1
```

A cursory, global check can also be done of the system-level wait events to get an idea of the I/O bottlenecks that may be occurring. A script like the *syswaits.sql* script can be used to perform such a check:

🖫 **syswaits.sql**

```
select
   event,
   total_waits,
   round(100 * (total_waits / sum_waits),2) pct_waits,
   time_wait_sec,
   round(100 * (time_wait_sec / greatest(sum_time_waited,1)),2)
   pct_time_waited,
   total_timeouts,
   round(100 * (total_timeouts / greatest(sum_timeouts,1)),2)
   pct_timeouts,
   average_wait_sec
from
(select
      event,
      total_waits,
      round((time_waited / 100),2) time_wait_sec,
      total_timeouts,
      round((average_wait / 100),2) average_wait_sec
from
      sys.v_$system_event
where
      event not in
('lock element cleanup',
 'pmon timer',
 'rdbms ipc message',
 'rdbms ipc reply',
 'smon timer',
 'SQL*Net message from client',
 'SQL*Net break/reset to client',
 'SQL*Net message to client',
 'SQL*Net more data from client',
 'dispatcher timer',
 'Null event',
 'parallel query dequeue wait',
 'parallel query idle wait - Slaves',
 'pipe get',
```

```
'PL/SQL lock timer',
'slave wait',
'virtual circuit status',
'WMON goes to sleep') and
event not like 'DFS%' and
event not like 'KXFX%'),
(select
        sum(total_waits) sum_waits,
        sum(total_timeouts) sum_timeouts,
        sum(round((time_waited / 100),2)) sum_time_waited
from
        sys.v_$system_event
where
        event not in
('lock element cleanup',
'pmon timer',
'rdbms ipc message',
'rdbms ipc reply',
'smon timer',
'SQL*Net message from client',
'SQL*Net break/reset to client',
'SQL*Net message to client',
'SQL*Net more data from client',
'dispatcher timer',
'Null event',
'parallel query dequeue wait',
'parallel query idle wait - Slaves',
'pipe get',
'PL/SQL lock timer',
'slave wait',
'virtual circuit status',
'WMON goes to sleep') and
event not like 'DFS%' and
event not like 'KXFX%')
order by
  2 desc, 1 asc;
```

Output from this query could resemble something like this:

	EVENT	TOTAL_WAITS	PCT_WAITS	TIME_WAIT_SEC	PCT_TIME_WAITED	TOTAL_TIMEOUTS	PCT_TIMEOUTS	AVERAGE_WAIT_SEC
1	control file parallel write	13763	66.1	11.8	43.77	0	0	0
2	direct path write	2216	10.64	4.18	15.5	0	0	0
3	db file sequential read	1874	9	1.76	6.53	0	0	0
4	control file sequential read	1805	8.67	3.86	14.32	0	0	0
5	direct path read	319	1.53	1.11	4.12	0	0	0
6	refresh controlfile command	231	1.11	1.7	6.31	0	0	.01
7	log file parallel write	165	.79	.1	.37	0	0	0
8	db file scattered read	130	.62	.11	.41	0	0	0
9	file open	130	.62	.75	2.78	0	0	.01
10	log file sync	51	.24	.5	1.85	0	0	.01
11	db file parallel write	46	.22	.39	1.45	0	0	.01
12	file identify	35	.17	.06	.22	0	0	0
13	latch free	22	.11	.52	1.93	21	100	.02
14	library cache pin	12	.06	0	0	0	0	0
15	buffer busy waits	10	.05	.12	.45	0	0	.01
16	log file sequential read	5	.02	0	0	0	0	0
17	log file single write	5	.02	0	0	0	0	0
18	instance state change	1	0	0	0	0	0	0
19	library cache load lock	1	0	0	0	0	0	0
20	reliable message	1	0	0	0	0	0	0

Figure 5.7: *System Event Waits Output*

A few quick things to note about the output from the waits SQL script:

- Numerous waits for the *db file scattered read* event may indicate a problem with table scans.

- Many waits for the *latch free* event could indicate excessive amounts of logical I/O activity.

- High wait times for the *enqueue* event pinpoints a problem with lock contention.

Once there is a feel for the I/O numbers at a global level, begin to work one's way further down into what is really going on under the covers.

Determine Global Object Access Patterns

Oracle has come a long way in helping the database professional determine how objects in the database are being accessed. Oracle 9i, in particular, has introduced some wonderful new statistical views that can be queried to get a handle on object access patterns. If the move has not been made up to 9i yet, do not worry, as there are still methods that can be used to understand the I/O occurring against the database.

Begin with a global sweep of access pattern activity. A query such as the *globaccpatt.sql* script can be used for that:

```
select
   name,
   value
from
   sys.v_$sysstat
where
   name in
   ('table scans (cache partitions)',
    'table scans (direct read)',
    'table scans (long tables)',
    'table scans (rowid ranges)',
    'table scans (short tables)',
    'table fetch by rowid',
    'table fetch continued row')
order by
   1;
```

Results from such a query might look like this:

```
NAME                                VALUE
----------------------------------------
table fetch by rowid                146540
table fetch continued row              698
table scans (cache partitions)           0
table scans (direct read)                0
table scans (long tables)                0
table scans (rowid ranges)               0
table scans (short tables)             262
```

When reviewing the output from the above query, focus on these things: large-table full-table scans can indicate suboptimal SQL and/or missing indexes, and cases where the SQL needlessly reads all blocks in the table.

Examine Storage-level Statistics

Understanding where the storage-level hot spots of a database are is beneficial for a couple of reasons:

- A feel for overworked physical disks can be obtained by viewing I/O statistics at the tablespace and datafile levels. If a particular disk or set of disks is under too much strain, either relocate the tablespaces to less-used devices or create new tablespaces on different disks and move hot objects onto them (assuming, of course, there are extra disks available).

- If standard DBA practice has been followed and indexes have been placed in the particular tablespace, the I/O statistics can be viewed for that tablespace and see if the indexes are actually being used:

🖫 fileio.sql

```
select
    d.name file_name,
    c.name tablespace_name,
    b.phyrds,
    b.phywrts,
    b.phyblkrd,
    b.phyblkwrt,
    b.readtim,
    b.writetim
from
    sys.v_$datafile a,
    sys.v_$filestat b,
    sys.ts$ c,
    sys.v_$dbfile d,
    sys.file$ e
where
    a.file# = b.file#
and
    a.file# = d.file#
and
    e.ts# = c.ts#
and
    e.file# = d.file#
union all
select
    v.fnnam file_name,
    c.name tablespace_name,
    b.phyrds,
    b.phywrts,
    b.phyblkrd,
    b.phyblkwrt,
    b.readtim,
    b.writetim
from
    sys.v_$tempfile a,
    sys.v_$tempstat b,
    sys.ts$ c,
    sys.x$kccfn v,
    sys.x$ktfthc hc
where
    a.file# = b.file#
and
    a.file# = hc.ktfthctfno
and
    hc.ktfthctsn = c.ts#
and
    v.fntyp = 7
and
    v.fnnam is not null
and
    v.fnfno = hc.ktfthctfno
```

```
and
   hc.ktfthctsn = c.ts#
order by
   3 desc;
```

Output from one of the previous queries would look like this:

	FILE_NAME	TABLESPACE_NAME	PHYRDS	PHYWRTS	PHYBLKRD	PHYBLKWRT	READTIM	WRITETIM
1	D:\ORACLE\ORA92\O92\SYSTEM01.DBF	SYSTEM	22735	1318	29987	1318	6581	331
2	D:\ORACLE\ORA92\O92\XDB01.DBF	XDB	2979	2	2990	2	850	5
3	D:\ORACLE\ORA92\O92\OEM_REPOSITORY.DBF	OEM_REPOSITORY	1582	2	1582	2	487	5
4	D:\ORACLE\ORA92\O92\USERS01.DBF	USERS	554	55	619	55	213	20
5	D:\ORACLE\ORA92\O92\DRSYS01.DBF	DRSYS	282	2	282	2	129	3
6	D:\ORACLE\ORA92\O92\TOOLS01.DBF	TOOLS	84	0	84	0	48	0
7	D:\ORACLE\ORA92\O92\UNDOTBS01.DBF	UNDOTBS1	46	8567	46	8567	709	484
8	D:\ORACLE\ORA92\O92\INDX01.DBF	INDX	11	2	11	2	49	5
9	D:\ORACLE\ORA92\O92\AUTOSEG.ORA	AUTOSEG	6	2	6	2	24	2

Figure 5.8: *Datafile and Tablespace I/O Details*

Some areas to consider when viewing the output of these queries:

- A lot of activity in the SYSTEM tablespace and datafiles may indicate a lot of recursive calls such as space management and more. Temporary tablespaces which are devoted to sort activity and therefore, showing higher volumes of physical I/O, could indicate a problem with excessive disk activity.

- Quickly review all the physical I/O for each drive/file system and get a feel for the overworked disks on the server. If there are underutilized disk drives with their own controllers, then consider relocating some tablespaces that exhibit high I/O characteristics to those drives.

Locating Hot I/O Objects

Once the location of the hotspots in the database is known with respect to storage structures, it is time to drill further down and locate the objects that are the most in demand. There is no doubt that hub tables in a system can cause a major I/O bottleneck if they are not correctly designed and implemented.

To get an idea of which objects have been the favorite of a database's SQL calls, run the following *toptables.sql* query which gets the top 100 objects as determined by SQL statement execution:

💾 **toptables.sql**

```
select
   table_owner "table owner",
   table_name "table name",
   command "command issued",
   0 - executions   "executions",
   disk_reads "disk reads",
   gets "buffer gets",
   rows_processed "rows processed"
from
(select
        distinct executions,
                command,
                table_owner,
                table_name,
                gets,
                rows_processed,
                disk_reads
 from
(select
        decode (a.command_type ,
                2, 'insert ' ,
                3,'select ',
                6, 'update   ' ,
                7, 'delete ' ,
                26,'table lock  ') command ,
                c.owner table_owner,
                c.name table_name ,
                sum(a.disk_reads) disk_reads  ,
                sum(0 - a.executions) executions ,
                sum(a.buffer_gets) gets   ,
                sum(a.rows_processed) rows_processed
 from
        sys.v_$sql  a ,
        sys.v_$object_dependency b ,
        sys.v_$db_object_cache   c
 where
        a.command_type in (2,3,6,7,26)and
        b.from_address = a.address and
        b.to_owner = c.owner and
        b.to_name= c.name and
        c.type = 'table' and
        c.owner not in ('SYS','SYSTEM')
 group by
        a.command_type , c.owner  , c.name )  )
where
        rownum <= 100;
```

Output from the above query might look like this:

Figure 5.9: *Top Tables Query Output*

	TABLE OWNER	TABLE NAME	COMMAND ISSUED	EXECUTIONS	DISK READS	BUFFER GETS	ROWS PROCESSED
1	ERADMIN	TESTXML_927	SELECT	13	2	131	0
2	ERADMIN	ADMISSION	SELECT	7	13	184	2508
3	ERADMIN	TESTXML_927NEW2	SELECT	4	0	94	0
4	ERADMIN	TESTLOB_NEW	SELECT	2	5	127	2
5	ERADMIN	ADMISSION_TEST	SELECT	1	1	111	0
6	ERADMIN	MEDICATION_DISP	SELECT	1	1	32	0
7	ERADMIN	PATIENT_PROCEDURE	SELECT	1	5	23	0
8	ERADMIN	TESTXML_927NEW	SELECT	1	0	53	3
9	WMSYS	WM$ENV_VARS	SELECT	1	8	403	1
10	WMSYS	WM$VERSIONED_TABLES	SELECT	1	8	403	1
11	WMSYS	WM$VERSION_HIERARCHY_TABLE	SELECT	1	8	403	1

Observing a single table with a lot of DML activity provides a clue that it may be a potential bottleneck for the system. Other things to consider when reviewing output from this query include:

- Small, frequently accessed tables should be considered candidates for the Oracle KEEP buffer pool.

- Large tables that are often accessed and scanned should be reviewed to determine if they could be partitioned. Partitioning can reduce scan times if only one or a handful of partitions can be scanned instead of the entire table.

- High amounts of disk reads for tables in the above query are red flags that can help identify partitioning possibilities.

If large tables are suspected of being scanned and Oracle 9i is being used, make use of the new *v_$sql_plan* view to validate these suspicions. The *largescan9i.sql* query uses this new view to show which large tables, defined in the query as tables over 1MB, are being scanned in the database:

🖫 **largescan.sql**

```
select
    table_owner,
    table_name,
    table_type,
    size_kb,
    statement_count,
    reference_count,
    executions,
    executions * reference_count total_scans
```

Troubleshooting I/O Hotspots

```
from
   (select
       a.object_owner table_owner,
       a.object_name table_name,
       b.segment_type table_type,
       b.bytes / 1024 size_kb,
       sum(c.executions ) executions,
       count( distinct a.hash_value ) statement_count,
       count( * ) reference_count
   from
       sys.v_$sql_plan a,
       sys.dba_segments b,
       sys.v_$sql c
   where
       a.object_owner (+) = b.owner
   and
       a.object_name (+) = b.segment_name
and
       b.segment_type IN ('TABLE', 'TABLE PARTITION')
and
       a.operation LIKE '%TABLE%'
and
       a.options = 'FULL'
and
       a.hash_value = c.hash_value
and
       b.bytes / 1024 > 1024
group by
   a.object_owner,
   a.object_name,
   a.operation,
   b.bytes / 1024,
   b.segment_type
order by
   4 desc, 1, 2 );
```

	TABLE_OWNER	TABLE_NAME	TABLE_TYPE	SIZE_KB	STATEMENT_COUNT	REFERENCE_COUNT	EXECUTIONS	TOTAL_SCANS
1	ERADMIN	EMP	TABLE	19456	2	2	2	4
2	SYS	DEPENDENCY$	TABLE	3496	1	1	1	1
3	SYS	OBJ$	TABLE	3136	4	7	25	175

Figure 5.10: *Output from the Large-table Scan Query*

After finding out what table is being accessed the most, next move into finding out who is causing all the activity.

Find the Current I/O Session Bandits

If the complaint of poor performance is ongoing, check connected sessions to see which users are impacting the system in undesirable ways.

First, get an idea of the percentage that each session is/has taken up with respect to I/O. One rule of thumb is that if any session is currently consuming 50% or more of the total I/O, then that session and its SQL need to be investigated further to determine what activity it is engaged in.

If the concern is just with physical I/O, then the *physpctio.sql* query will provide the information needed:

🖫 **physpctio.sql**

```
select
   sid,
   username,
   round(100 * total_user_io/total_io,2) tot_io_pct
from
(select
     b.sid sid,
     nvl(b.username,p.name) username,
     sum(value) total_user_io
 from
     sys.v_$statname c,
     sys.v_$sesstat a,
     sys.v_$session b,
     sys.v_$bgprocess p
 where
     a.statistic#=c.statistic# and
     p.paddr (+) = b.paddr and
     b.sid=a.sid and
     c.name in ('physical reads',
                'physical writes',
                'physical writes direct',
                'physical reads direct',
                'physical writes direct (lob)',
                'physical reads direct (lob)')
group by
     b.sid, nvl(b.username,p.name)),
(select
     sum(value) total_io
 from
     sys.v_$statname c,
     sys.v_$sesstat a
 where
     a.statistic#=c.statistic# and
     c.name in ('physical reads',
                'physical writes',
                'physical writes direct',
                'physical reads direct',
                'physical writes direct (lob)',
                'physical reads direct (lob)'))
order by
     3 desc;
```

If seeing the total I/O picture is desired, meaning both logical and physical I/O, then use the *totpctio.sql* query instead:

💾 totpctio.sql

```
select
      SID,
      USERNAME,
      ROUND(100 * TOTAL_USER_IO/TOTAL_IO,2) TOT_IO_PCT
from
(select
      b.SID SID,
      nvl(b.USERNAME,p.NAME) USERNAME,
      SUM(VALUE) TOTAL_USER_IO
from
    sys.V_$STATNAME c,
    sys.V_$SESSTAT a,
    sys.V_$SESSION b,
    sys.v_$bgprocess p
where
      a.STATISTIC#=c.STATISTIC# and
      p.paddr (+) = b.paddr and
      b.SID=a.SID and
      c.NAME in ('physical reads','physical writes',
                'consistent changes','consistent gets',
                'db block gets','db block changes',
                'physical writes direct',
                'physical reads direct',
                'physical writes direct (lob)',
                'physical reads direct (lob)')
group by
      b.SID, nvl(b.USERNAME,p.name)),
(select
      sum(value) TOTAL_IO
from
      sys.V_$STATNAME c,
      sys.V_$SESSTAT a
where
      a.STATISTIC#=c.STATISTIC# and
      c.NAME in ('physical reads','physical writes',
                'consistent changes',
                'consistent gets','db block gets',
                'db block changes',
                'physical writes direct',
                'physical reads direct',
                'physical writes direct (lob)',
                'physical reads direct (lob)'))
order by
      3 DESC;
```

Regardless of which query is being used, the output might resemble something like the following:

```
SID   USERNAME        TOT_IO_PCT
--------------------------------------
9     USR1                71.26
20    SYS                 15.76
5     SMON                 7.11
2     DBWR                 4.28
12    SYS                  1.42
6     RECO                  .12
7     SNP0                  .01
10    SNP3                  .01
11    SNP4                  .01
8     SNP1                  .01
1     PMON                    0
3     ARCH                    0
4     LGWR                    0
```

In the above example, it would be prudent to examine the USR1 session to see what SQL calls they are making. The above queries are excellent weapons that can be used to quickly pinpoint problem I/O sessions.

If more detail with respect to the top I/O session in a database is required, use the rather large *topiousers.sql* query instead to see all the actual I/O numbers:

topiousers.sql

```
select
       b.sid sid,
       decode (b.username,null,e.name,b.username)
user_name,
       d.spid os_id,
       b.machine machine_name,
       to_char(logon_time,'mm/dd/yy hh:mi:ss pm')
logon_time,
       (sum(decode(c.name,'physical reads',value,0))
+
sum(decode(c.name,'physical writes',value,0))
+
sum(decode(c.name,
'physical writes direct',value,0)) +
sum(decode(c.name,
'physical writes direct (lob)',value,0)) +
sum(decode(c.name,
'physical reads direct (lob)',value,0)) +
sum(decode(c.name,
'physical reads direct',value,0)))
total_physical_io,
       (sum(decode(c.name,'db block gets',value,0))
+
sum(decode(c.name,
'db block changes',value,0))  +
sum(decode(c.name,'consistent changes',value,0)) +
sum(decode(c.name,'consistent gets',value,0))  )
```

```
   total_logical_io,
   100 - 100 *(round ((sum (decode
   (c.name, 'physical reads', value, 0)) -
   sum (decode (c.name,
   'physical reads direct', value, 0))) /
   (sum (decode (c.name, 'db block gets',
   value, 1)) +
   sum (decode (c.name, 'consistent gets',
   value, 0))),3)) hit_ratio,
   sum(decode(c.name,'sorts (disk)',value,0))
   disk_sorts,
   sum(decode(c.name,'sorts (memory)',value,0))
   memory_sorts,
   sum(decode(c.name,'sorts (rows)',value,0))
   rows_sorted,
   sum(decode(c.name,'user commits',value,0))
   commits,
   sum(decode(c.name,'user rollbacks',value,0))
   rollbacks,
   sum(decode(c.name,'execute count',value,0))
   executions,
   sum(decode(c.name,'physical reads',value,0))
   physical_reads,
   sum(decode(c.name,'db block gets',value,0))
   db_block_gets,
   sum(decode(c.name,'consistent gets',value,0))
   consistent_gets,
   sum(decode(c.name,'consistent changes',value,0))
   consistent_changes
from
   sys.v_$sesstat a,
   sys.v_$session b,
   sys.v_$statname c,
   sys.v_$process d,
   sys.v_$bgprocess e
where
   a.statistic#=c.statistic#
and
   b.sid=a.sid
and
   d.addr = b.paddr
and
   e.paddr (+) = b.paddr
and
   c.name in
   ('physical reads',
   'physical writes',
   'physical writes direct',
   'physical reads direct',
   'physical writes direct (lob)',
   'physical reads direct (lob)',
   'db block gets',
   'db block changes',
   'consistent changes',
   'consistent gets',
   'sorts (disk)',
   'sorts (memory)',
   'sorts (rows)',
   'user commits',
```

```
     'user rollbacks',
     'execute count'
)
group by
   b.sid,
   d.spid,
   decode (b.username,null,e.name,b.username),
          b.machine,
          to_char(logon_time,'mm/dd/yy hh:mi:ss pm')
order by
   6 desc;
```

Output from the query above could look like the following:

	SID	USER_NAME	OS_ID	MACHINE_NAME	LOGON_TIME	TOTAL_PHYSICAL_IO	TOTAL_LOGICAL_IO	HIT_RATIO	DISK_SORTS	MEMORY_SORTS	ROWS_SORTED	COMMIT
1	2	DBW0	1064	EBT2K11	12/05/02 03:12:10 PM	9982	0	100	0	0	0	
2	12	ORA_MONITOR	2488	EBT2K\EBT2K08	12/12/02 05:28:18 PM	8527	59015775	100	0	289379	126302548	
3	5	SMON	296	EBT2K11	12/05/02 03:12:11 PM	2657	465527	99.4	0	78	175	
4	3	LGWR	980	EBT2K11	12/05/02 03:12:10 PM	34	0	100	0	0	0	
5	6	RECO	1220	EBT2K11	12/05/02 03:12:11 PM	1	1753	99.9	0	8	48	
6	1	PMON	1032	EBT2K11	12/05/02 03:12:09 PM	0	0	100	0	0	0	
7	4	CKPT	1144	EBT2K11	12/05/02 03:12:10 PM	0	0	100	0	0	0	
8	16	SYS	3956	EBT2K\ROBINWS	12/17/02 04:55:29 PM	0	4	100	0	0	0	
9	11	SYS	3096	EBT2K\ROBINWS	12/17/02 05:26:31 PM	0	235	100	0	66	27449	

Figure 5.11: *Sample Top I/O Users Detail Output*

Such a query can provide details about the actual, raw I/O numbers for each connected session. Armed with this information, begin to drill down into each heavy-hitting I/O session to determine what SQL calls they are making and which sets of SQL are the I/O hogs.

While how to troubleshoot I/O from a user standpoint is now known, it is best not to forget about all the system activity that is caused by Oracle itself.

Miscellaneous I/O Considerations

Before leaving the topic of I/O hotspots, there are a couple of remaining items to mention in passing: examining background processes and monitoring rollback activity.

Examining Background Processes

How can it be seen whether Oracle's DBWR, LGWR, ARCH or other background processes are experiencing I/O bottlenecks or not? First, issue the *bgact.sql* query to get a general handle on DBWR and LGWR activity:

💾 **bgact.sql**

```
select
   name,
   value
from
   sys.v_$sysstat
where
   (name like '%DBWR%'
or
    name in
       ('dirty buffers inspected',
        'summed dirty queue length',
        'write requests'))
Or
        (name like '%redo%')
order by
     1;
```

The output from the above query might look like this:

```
NAME                                    VALUE
- - - - - - - - - - - - - - - - - - - - - - - - - - - - - - - - - - - - -
DBWR buffers scanned                      0
DBWR checkpoint buffers written         438
DBWR checkpoints                          0
DBWR cross instance writes                0
DBWR free buffers found                   0
DBWR lru scans                            0
DBWR make free requests                   0
DBWR revisited being-written buffer       0
DBWR summed scan depth                    0
DBWR transaction table writes           151
DBWR undo block writes                  154
dirty buffers inspected                   0
redo blocks written                     804
redo buffer allocation retries            0
redo entries                           1297
redo log space requests                   0
redo log space wait time                  0
redo log switch interrupts                0
redo ordering marks                       0
redo size                            329192
redo synch time                          54
redo synch writes                       116
redo wastage                          69528
redo write time                          79
redo writer latching time                 0
redo writes                             237
summed dirty queue length                 0
```

Seeing non-zero values for the DBWR summed dirty queue length typically indicates that buffers are being left in the write queue after a write request. This could signal that the DBWR process is falling behind and that more DBWR processes should be added to the system. Non-zero values for the redo log space wait requests and redo log space wait time statistics could indicate a too-low setting for the log buffer.

Archive log I/O problems can usually be viewed in the form of entries in the Oracle alert log, as in messages indicating waits for the archive log files to complete. An idea of how many logs the archive process writes per day can be obtained by issuing a query like the *archhist.sql* script, which shows the number of logs written per day for the last 30 days:

🖫 archhist.sql

```
select
    to_char(completion_time,'mm/dd/yy')  completion_time,
    count(*)                             log_count
from
    sys.v_$archived_log
where
    sysdate - completion_time < 31
group by
    to_char(completion_time,'mm/dd/yy')
order by
    1 desc;
```

Once the overall I/O picture of Oracle's background processes is clear, then begin to move into specific areas like rollback segments.

Troubleshooting Rollback Activity

Rollback segments can become hotspots for I/O activity, especially if a lot of DML activity is occurring in the database. Oracle writes data to individual rollback segments to undo changes made to the Oracle database from within a transaction. Rollbacks are also used to maintain read consistency for multiple users of modified data.

To check the amount of rollback I/O the database is experiencing, use the *rolldet.sql* query:

rolldet.sql

```sql
select
  name,
  round ((rssize / 1024), 2) size_kb,
  shrinks,
  extends,
  gets,
  waits,
  writes,
  xacts,
  status,
  round ((hwmsize / 1024), 2) hw_kb
from
  sys.v_$rollstat a,
  sys.v_$rollname b
where
  (a.usn = b.usn)
order by
  name;
```

Here is a sample of the output:

	NAME	SIZE_KB	SHRINKS	EXTENDS	GETS	WAITS	WRITES	XACTS	STATUS	HW_KB
1	RBS0	4088	0	0	3572	0	3624	0	ONLINE	4088
2	RBS1	4088	0	0	3573	0	6194	0	ONLINE	4088
3	RBS10	4088	0	0	3569	0	8252	0	ONLINE	4088
4	RBS11	4088	0	0	3568	0	1650	0	ONLINE	4088
5	RBS12	4088	0	0	3566	0	1266	0	ONLINE	4088
6	RBS13	4088	0	0	3566	0	1150	0	ONLINE	4088
7	RBS14	4088	0	0	3566	0	1420	0	ONLINE	4088
8	RBS15	4088	0	0	3566	0	1152	0	ONLINE	4088
9	RBS16	4088	0	0	3566	0	1480	0	ONLINE	4088
10	RBS17	4088	0	0	3566	0	4448	0	ONLINE	4088
11	RBS18	4088	0	0	3566	0	1436	0	ONLINE	4088
12	RBS19	4088	0	0	3567	0	4266	0	ONLINE	4088
13	RBS2	4088	0	0	3575	0	3874	0	ONLINE	4088
14	RBS20	4088	0	0	3566	0	994	0	ONLINE	4088
15	RBS21	4088	0	0	3566	0	1054	0	ONLINE	4088
16	RBS22	4088	0	0	3566	0	1044	0	ONLINE	4088
17	RBS23	4088	0	0	3566	0	1214	0	ONLINE	4088
18	RBS24	4088	0	0	3568	0	1556	0	ONLINE	4088
19	RBS25	4088	0	0	3568	0	1528	0	ONLINE	4088

Figure 5.12: *Rollback Activity Details*

To properly tune rollback I/O, first make sure that there are enough segments to accommodate the workload of the database. Constantly seeing a count of active rollback segments equal to or near the number of rollbacks defined for the database is an indicator that more should be created.

An overall rollback contention ratio of 1% or higher is an indicator of too few rollbacks as well. Seeing wait counts greater than zero for each rollback segment is further evidence that more rollback segments should be created. If Oracle 9i is being used, then make use of the new UNDO tablespace feature that allows Oracle to automatically manage all rollback activity, including dynamically allocating more rollback segments when it becomes necessary.

After ensuring that enough rollback segments exist in the database, turn attention to the question of sizing. Dynamic rollback extension can take a toll on performance if segments are consistently enlarged to accommodate heavy transaction loads. Seeing rollback segments undergoing numerous extends and shrinks as Oracle returns a segment back to its optimal setting, as well as rollback segments with current or high watermark sizes greater than their optimal setting, usually is a good indicator that they should be permanently enlarged.

It is certainly not easy keeping track of all the I/O activity in a heavy-duty database, but by following the roadmap provided in this chapter and using the included scripts, all the hotspots in any Oracle database that are being managed should be quickly uncovered.

By starting with global I/O statistics and moving through I/O at the storage structure, object, and user levels, it can quickly be determined where the I/O hotspots are and then start working to make things better.

Summary

Issues with the shared pool in Oracle databases were covered in this chapter. The shared pool helps Oracle keep these reference-related activities to a minimum by holding SQL statements, along with code and object definitions, in memory. Several scripts were given that showed the consequences of an undersized or oversized shared pool. Troubleshooting the log buffer, which caches redo entries prior to writing them to disk, as well as sort operations were also examined. The chapter wrapped up with issues regarding with latches and dealt extensively with troubleshooting I/O hotspots by identifying the objects and users that are responsible for the most I/O issues.

The next chapter will look at how the major bottlenecks in the system can be eliminated by using both wait-based and extended analytical techniques.

Troubleshooting Problem Sessions

Troubleshooting Problem Sessions

It is an old joke among database administrators that databases would run just fine if no users were allowed to connect to them. Of course this is not the case, and with the internet-enabled database applications, it is possible to have databases with virtually no limit to the number of users that can connect to the system. Also, as user load increases, there is an increased need to manage the performance of the database with respect to user and code activity.

Today, the bar has been raised for high-usage databases. It is not uncommon to see large eCommerce systems that support thousands of transactions per second, and many of these databases have strict service level agreements (SLAs) mandating sub-second response time. The DBA's performance strategy should include solid techniques for quickly identifying database sessions that are using excessive resources or causing system bottlenecks. It was shown earlier that it is best to use ratio-based and bottleneck analysis techniques when troubleshooting Oracle databases.

When session and SQL activity is being examined, use a third analytic technique referred to as workload analysis. This chapter will cover how to perform workload analysis by looking at session activity using a variety of analysis techniques and scripts.

The main topics to be covered are:

- Finding storage hogs

- Locating top resource sessions
- Pinpointing sessions with problem SQL

Begin by looking at security holes because the user accounts that belong on a system should be the only ones that are actually there.

Finding Storage Hogs

One thing that should be kept track of in the database is the amount of storage space that each user account is consuming. It is not uncommon for developers to create object backups of their object backups when working on a critical project, and if those objects are left indefinitely in the database, there might be a lot of unusable space that may be needed at a later time.

A good query to run to see how much space each user account has consumed is the *totuserspace.sql* script:

🖫 totuserspace.sql

```
select
        owner,
        round((byte_count / 1024 / 1024),2) space_used_mb,
        round(100 * (byte_count / tot_bytes),2) pct_of_database
from
(select
        owner ,
        sum(bytes) as byte_count
from
        sys.dba_segments
where
        segment_type not in ('TEMPORARY','CACHE')
group by
        owner
order by
        2 desc),
(select
        sum(bytes) as tot_bytes
from
        sys.dba_segments);
```

Partial output from the above query might look something like this:

```
OWNER          SPACE_USED_MB    PCT_OF_DATABASE
------------   -------------    ---------------
ERADMIN              807.10              58.48
SYS                  322.36              23.36
USER1                 45.47               3.29
REPO                  27.19               1.97
SYSTEM                22.88               1.66
```

This script should be run periodically to see if any user accounts are hogging the majority of space in a database. Of course, some databases only have one schema account that contains application objects, so in that case there should not be anything to worry about. If, however, a number of accounts with large amounts of data have been noticed, check each user to ensure that bogus objects have not been left that both clutter up the user database files and add to the size of the Oracle data dictionary.

Another storage issue to examine from time to time is the amount of temporary space connected sessions are using. Many DBAs have experienced the sad fact that large disk sorts can cause out-of-space conditions to manifest quickly at both the database and operating system level. To get an idea of historical temporary tablespace (sort) usage, execute the *sortusage.sql* query:

💾 **sortusage.sql**

```
select
        tablespace_name,
        current_users,
        total_extents,
        used_extents,
        free_extents,
        max_used_size,
        max_sort_size
from
        sys.v_$sort_segment
order by 1;
```

Figure 6.1: *Output From the Sortusage.sql Query*

The output will tell how many users are currently using space in each temporary tablespace along with the current used extent and free extent numbers. The last two columns will tell the largest number of total extents ever used for all sorts and the size of the single largest sort in extents since the database has been up.

Such knowledge can help with a plan involving the size of the temporary tablespace(s). Many DBAs will size their temporary tablespaces very large in anticipation of heavy sort activity only to find that such sorts do not occur. If heavy temporary tablespace usage is not seen, the temporary tablespace datafiles may possibly be resized and space reclaimed on the server.

If the *sortusage* query shows that users are currently using space in a temporary tablespace, it may be necessary to dig deeper and see exactly what they are doing. The *sortdet.sql* query can give this exact detail.

```
sortdet.sql
select
        sql_text,
        sid,
        c.username,
        machine,
        tablespace,
        extents,
        blocks
from
        sys.v_$sort_usage a,
        sys.v_$sqlarea b,
        sys.v_$session c
where
        a.sqladdr = b.address and
        a.sqlhash = b.hash_value and
        a.session_addr = c.saddr
order by
        sid;
```

Output from the previous query might look like this:

SQL_TEXT	SID	USERNAME	MACHINE	TABLESPACE	EXTENTS	BLOCKS
SELECT * FROM	10	ERADMIN	ROBS	TEMP	10	80

Using this query, the SQL call, current session information, and details on how much temporary space the SQL call is using can be obtained.

Red flags should begin to run up the flagpole if continuous large disk sorts are occurring on the system.

Sort activity that occurs on disk is much slower than sorts that occur in memory, so begin to examine the memory settings, as well as the SQL statements that are uncovered from this query, to see if unnecessary sorts are occurring or if the *init.ora/spfile* parameters relating to sorting are set too low.

Locating Top Resource Sessions

When the phone starts ringing with complaints of performance slowdowns, one of the first things that should be performed is a cursory examination of the workload that exists on the database. This is done by checking:

- What sessions are connected to the database

- What and how much resources each session is using

- What the resource-heavy sessions are/have been executing

There are a number of database monitors on the market that give a "top sessions" view of system activity. Even if there is not a third-party monitor at the DBA's disposal, all the various metrics that will be needed can be quickly pinpointed with just a few queries.

To get a bird's eye view of the top resource users with respect to physical I/O, logical I/O, memory, and CPU, execute the rather large *topsess.sql* query:

🖫 **topsess.sql**

```
select
       'top physical i/o process' category,
       sid,
       username,
       total_user_io amt_used,
       round(100 * total_user_io/total_io,2) pct_used
from
(select
       b.sid sid,
       nvl(b.username,p.name) username,
       sum(value) total_user_io
```

```
from
     sys.v_$statname c,
     sys.v_$sesstat a,
     sys.v_$session b,
     sys.v_$bgprocess p
where
     a.statistic#=c.statistic# and
     p.paddr (+) = b.paddr and
     b.sid=a.sid and
     c.name in ('physical reads','physical writes',
               'physical reads direct',
               'physical reads direct (lob)',
               'physical writes direct',
               'physical writes direct (lob)')
group by
     b.sid, nvl(b.username,p.name)
order by
     3 desc),
(select
     sum(value) total_io
from
     sys.v_$statname c,
     sys.v_$sesstat a
where
     a.statistic#=c.statistic# and
     c.name in ('physical reads','physical writes',
               'physical reads direct',
               'physical reads direct (lob)',
               'physical writes direct',
               'physical writes direct (lob)'))
where
     rownum < 2
union all
select
     'top logical i/o process',
     sid,
     username,
     total_user_io amt_used,
     round(100 * total_user_io/total_io,2) pct_used
from
(select
     b.sid sid,
     nvl(b.username,p.name) username,
     sum(value) total_user_io
from
     sys.v_$statname c,
     sys.v_$sesstat a,
     sys.v_$session b,
     sys.v_$bgprocess p
where
     a.statistic#=c.statistic# and
     p.paddr (+) = b.paddr and
     b.sid=a.sid and
     c.name in ('consistent gets','db block gets')
group by
     b.sid, nvl(b.username,p.name)
order by
     3 desc),
(select
```

```
      sum(value) total_io
from
      sys.v_$statname c,
      sys.v_$sesstat a
where
      a.statistic#=c.statistic# and
      c.name in ('consistent gets','db block gets'))
where
      rownum < 2
union all
select
      'top memory process',
      sid,
      username,
      total_user_mem,
      round(100 * total_user_mem/total_mem,2)
from
(select
      b.sid sid,
      nvl(b.username,p.name) username,
      sum(value) total_user_mem
from
      sys.v_$statname c,
      sys.v_$sesstat a,
      sys.v_$session b,
      sys.v_$bgprocess p
where
      a.statistic#=c.statistic# and
      p.paddr (+) = b.paddr and
      b.sid=a.sid and
      c.name in ('session pga memory','session uga memory')
group by
      b.sid, nvl(b.username,p.name)
order by
      3 desc),
(select
      sum(value) total_mem
from
      sys.v_$statname c,
      sys.v_$sesstat a
where
      a.statistic#=c.statistic# and
      c.name in ('session pga memory','session uga memory') )
where
      rownum < 2
union all
select
      'top cpu process',
      sid,
      username,
      total_user_cpu,
      round(100 * total_user_cpu/greatest(total_cpu,1),2)
from
(select
      b.sid sid,
      nvl(b.username,p.name) username,
      sum(value) total_user_cpu
from
      sys.v_$statname c,
```

```
        sys.v_$sesstat a,
        sys.v_$session b,
        sys.v_$bgprocess p
where
        a.statistic#=c.statistic# and
        p.paddr (+) = b.paddr and
        b.sid=a.sid and
        c.name = 'CPU used by this session'
group by
        b.sid, nvl(b.username,p.name)
order by
        3 desc),
(select
        sum(value) total_cpu
from
        sys.v_$statname c,
        sys.v_$sesstat a
where
        a.statistic#=c.statistic# and
        c.name = 'CPU used by this session'  )
where
        rownum < 2;
```

Output from this query might look like this:

```
CATEGORY                    SID   USERNAME  AMT_USED     PCT_USED
---------------------------------------------------------------
Top Physical I/O Process    19    ORA_USR1    120,423,120    99.68
Top Logical I/O Process      5    SMON          2,774,880    25.50
Top Memory Process          19    ORA_USR1      6,198,492    27.83
Top CPU Process             19    ORA_USR1     15,435,557    99.75
```

In the above example, focus on SID 19 as it seems to have a stranglehold on the system in terms of overall resource consumption. A rule of thumb is that no session should consume more than 25-50% of the overall resources in a particular category. If this is not the case, then examine each session in more detail to gain insight into what each might be doing.

To drill down and get more detail on across-the-board resource consumption, run a query such as the *topsessdet.sql* script.

topsessdet.sql

```
select *
        from
(select
        b.sid sid,
        decode (b.username,null,e.name,b.username) user_name,
        d.spid os_id,
        b.machine machine_name,
        to_char(logon_time,'mm/dd/yy hh:mi:ss pm') logon_time,
```

```
        (sum(decode(c.name,'physical reads',value,0)) +
        sum(decode(c.name,'physical writes',value,0)) +
        sum(decode(c.name,'physical writes direct',value,0)) +
        sum(decode(c.name,'physical writes direct (lob)',value,0))
        +
        sum(decode(c.name,'physical reads direct (lob)',value,0))
        +
        sum(decode(c.name,'physical reads direct',value,0)))
        total_physical_io,
        (sum(decode(c.name,'db block gets',value,0))  +
        sum(decode(c.name,'db block changes',value,0))  +
        sum(decode(c.name,'consistent changes',value,0)) +
        sum(decode(c.name,'consistent gets',value,0))  )
        total_logical_io,
        100 -
        100 *
        (round ((sum (decode (c.name, 'physical reads', value,
        0)) -
        sum (decode (c.name, 'physical reads direct', value,
        0))) /
        (sum (decode (c.name, 'db block gets', value, 1)) +
        sum (decode (c.name, 'consistent gets', value, 0))
        ),3)) hit_ratio,
        (sum(decode(c.name,'session pga memory',value,0))+
        sum(decode(c.name,'session uga memory',value,0))  )
        total_memory_usage,
        sum(decode(c.name,'parse count (total)',value,0)) parses,
        sum(decode(c.name,'CPU used by this session',value,0))
        total_cpu,
        sum(decode(c.name,'parse time cpu',value,0)) parse_cpu,
        sum(decode(c.name,'recursive cpu usage',value,0))
        recursive_cpu,
        sum(decode(c.name,'CPU used by this session',value,0)) -
        sum(decode(c.name,'parse time cpu',value,0)) -
        sum(decode(c.name,'recursive cpu usage',value,0))
        other_cpu,
        sum(decode(c.name,'sorts (disk)',value,0)) disk_sorts,
        sum(decode(c.name,'sorts (memory)',value,0)) memory_sorts,
        sum(decode(c.name,'sorts (rows)',value,0)) rows_sorted,
        sum(decode(c.name,'user commits',value,0)) commits,
        sum(decode(c.name,'user rollbacks',value,0)) rollbacks,
        sum(decode(c.name,'execute count',value,0)) executions,
        sum(decode(c.name,'physical reads',value,0))
        physical_reads,
        sum(decode(c.name,'db block gets',value,0)) db_block_gets,
        sum(decode(c.name,'consistent gets',value,0))
        consistent_gets,
        sum(decode(c.name,'consistent changes',value,0))
        consistent_changes
from
        sys.v_$sesstat a,
        sys.v_$session b,
        sys.v_$statname c,
        sys.v_$process d,
        sys.v_$bgprocess e
where
        a.statistic#=c.statistic# and
        b.sid=a.sid  and
        d.addr = b.paddr and
```

```
        e.paddr (+) = b.paddr  and
        c.name in ('physical reads',
                   'physical writes',
                   'physical writes direct',
                   'physical reads direct',
                   'physical writes direct (lob)',
                   'physical reads direct (lob)',
                   'db block gets',
                   'db block changes',
                   'consistent changes',
                   'consistent gets',
                   'session pga memory',
                   'session uga memory',
                   'parse count (total)',
                   'CPU used by this session',
                   'parse time cpu',
                   'recursive cpu usage',
                   'sorts (disk)',
                   'sorts (memory)',
                   'sorts (rows)',
                   'user commits',
                   'user rollbacks',
                   'execute count'
)
group by
        b.sid,
        d.spid,
        decode (b.username,null,e.name,b.username),
        b.machine,
        to_char(logon_time,'mm/dd/yy hh:mi:ss pm')
order by
        6 desc);
```

	SID	USER_NAME	OS_ID	MACHINE_NAME	LOGON_TIME	TOTAL_PHYSICAL_IO	TOTAL_LOGICAL_IO	HIT_RATIO	TOTAL_MEMORY_USAGE	PARSES	TOTAL_CPU	PARSE
1	13	USR1	344	EBT2K\EBT2K08	12/17/02 11:12:45 PM	7209	26147999	100	1646676	39406	52671	
2	2	DBMO	1484	EBT2K04	12/17/02 11:10:30 PM	762	0	100	758700	0	0	
3	5	SMON	2316	EBT2K04	12/17/02 11:10:31 PM	731	38035	98.1	282028	437	0	
4	18	SYS	2512	EBT2K\ROBINWS	12/18/02 01:44:59 PM	343	32345	100	541740	48	112	
5	3	LGWR	2492	EBT2K04	12/17/02 11:10:30 PM	66	0	100	302300	0	0	
6	4	CKPT	2580	EBT2K04	12/17/02 11:10:30 PM	64	0	100	358424	0	0	
7	15	DBSNMP	2304	EBT2K\EBT2K04	12/17/02 11:10:57 PM	37	349	89.9	192968	53	0	
8	12	SYS	2240	EBT2K\ROBINWS	12/18/02 04:26:29 PM	19	101	99.2	434232	20	5	
9	6	RECO	2404	EBT2K04	12/17/02 11:10:31 PM	1	162	99.5	154576	41	0	
10	1	PMON	2628	EBT2K04	12/17/02 11:10:29 PM	0	0	100	78220	0	0	
11	7	SNP0	2416	[NULL]	12/18/02 04:26:17 PM	0	0	100	367832	0	20	
12	8	SNP1	2040	[NULL]	12/18/02 04:26:18 PM	0	0	100	361780	0	14	
13	9	SNP2	2368	[NULL]	12/18/02 04:26:16 PM	0	0	100	214108	0	19	
14	10	SNP3	1868	[NULL]	12/18/02 04:26:17 PM	0	0	100	138300	0	6	
15	11	SNP4	2500	[NULL]	12/18/02 04:26:18 PM	0	0	100	138300	0	6	

Figure 6.2: *Partial Top Sessions Detail Output*

The output from this query is pretty large, but it can be seen from the selected columns that a lot more detail can be obtained from this query than the top session's summary query. For example, the CPU usage is broken down by parse, recursive, and other CPU usage.

Such details will help determine the exact nature of the work each session has been doing. Once the top sessions have been located, the next step is to locate the SQL calls they have made and determine what 'killer' queries each session has submitted. It may be a case of untuned SQL or inappropriately submitted SQL such as SQL used for a report that should be run during off hours.

The above queries and scripts are the traditional way of locating problem sessions in the database. However, there are some new techniques that can be used to uncover user sessions that might be contributing to an overall decrease in database performance. For example, many DBAs prefer to avoid the continuous scanning of large tables because of the heavy logical and physical I/O cost.

The currently connected sessions that are causing such scans can be located in a couple of different ways. The *userscans.sql* query can be used on Oracle to pick out the worst large-table scan offenders.

🖫 userscans.sql

```
select
      sid,
      username,
      total_user_scans,
      round(100 * total_user_scans/total_scans,2) pct_scans
from
(select
      b.sid sid,
      nvl(b.username,p.name) username,
      sum(value) total_user_scans
from
      sys.v_$statname c,
      sys.v_$sesstat a,
      sys.v_$session b,
      sys.v_$bgprocess p
where
      a.statistic#=c.statistic# and
      p.paddr (+) = b.paddr and
      b.sid=a.sid and
      c.name = 'table scans (long tables)'
group by
      b.sid,
      nvl(b.username,p.name)
order by
      3 desc),
(select
      sum(value) total_scans
from
```

```
      sys.v_$statname c,
      sys.v_$sesstat a
where
      a.statistic#=c.statistic# and

      c.name = 'table scans (long tables)');
```

Sample output from this query might look like this:

```
SID      USERNAME    TOTAL_USER_SCANS        PCT_SCANS
---------------------------------------------------
19   ORA_USER1   2286724                 99.94
5    SMON            1397                   .06
21   ERADMIN           47                     0
1    PMON               0                     0
```

Needless to say, if output has been received like that shown previously, there should not be too much trouble in identifying which SID had some explaining to do. Keep in mind that as a DBA, it is normal to focus on large-table scans vs. small-table scans. Often, Oracle can actually digest a small table much easier if it scans it rather than if it uses an index. Another way of getting a handle on sessions that are causing table scans is to look at wait events. The *db file scattered read* wait event is generally thought to be an indicator of table scan activity.

The *scatwait.sql* query will yield historical information regarding sessions that have caused *db file scattered read* wait events since the database has been up:

🖫 **scatwait.sql**

```
select
      b.sid,
      nvl(b.username,c.name) username,
      b.machine,
      a.total_waits,
      round((a.time_waited / 100),2)
      time_wait_sec,a.total_timeouts,
      round((average_wait / 100),2)
      average_wait_sec,
      round((a.max_wait / 100),2) max_wait_sec
  from
      sys.v_$session_event a,
      sys.v_$session b,
      sys.v_$bgprocess c
 where
      event = 'db file scattered read'
      and a.sid = b.sid
```

```
        and c.paddr (+) = b.paddr
order by
        3 desc,
        1 asc;
```

Again, it is not hard to find who the table scan glutton is on this system:

	SID	USERNAME	MACHINE	TOTAL_WAITS	TIME_WAIT_SEC	TOTAL_TIMEOUTS	AVERAGE_WAIT_SEC	MAX_WAIT_SEC
1	13	USR1	EBT2K\EBT2K08	16	.04	0	0	.01
2	5	SMON	EBT2K04	93	0	0	0	0

Figure 6.3: *Detailed Wait Output for Sessions with Possible Table Scans*

Note that the drawback of using the above query is that it cannot accurately be determined if the waits have been caused by small or large-table scans. While the above queries will work well on Oracle 8i and above, utilize some new *v$* views if Oracle 9i is being used. They give more flexibility identifying problem table scan situations.

The *large_scanusers.sql* query can help ferret out the parsing users submitting SQL calls that have scanned tables over 1MB.

```
large_scanusers.sql
select
        c.username username,
        count(a.hash_value) scan_count
from
    sys.v_$sql_plan a,
    sys.dba_segments b,
    sys.dba_users c,
    sys.v_$sql d
where
    a.object_owner (+) = b.owner
    and   a.object_name (+) = b.segment_name
    and   b.segment_type in ('TABLE', 'TABLE PARTITIOn')
    and   a.operation like '%TABLE%'
    and   a.options = 'FULL'
    and   c.user_id = d.parsing_user_id
    and   d.hash_value = a.hash_value
    and   b.bytes / 1024 > 1024
group by
      c.username
order by
      2 desc;
```

Output from such a query might look like this:

```
USERNAME      SCAN_COUNT
----------    ---------------
SYSTEM                     15
SYS                        13
ORA_USR1                    2
```

The above query to locate scans on larger tables can be tweaked by changing the *b.bytes / 1024 > 1024* clause. Large-table scans identified in the *v$sesstat* view are generally thought to be scans that were performed on a table of five blocks or greater.

The above query allows the flexibility to define 'large' in the DBA's own terms. However, regardless of what query is used, if sessions that appear to be causing a lot of table scans are found, the next step is to capture the SQL calls those sessions are issuing and begin the SQL examination/tuning process.

One final area to examine with respect to problem sessions that are using/holding resources is blocking locks. If the phone calls received about performance involve complaints about complete gridlock, it is a sure bet that a blocking lock situation exists. If it is suspected that this is the case, issue a few queries that should get right to the heart of the matter.

To get an idea if any blocking locks exist on the database, submit the *lockcnt.sql* query.

💾 lockcnt.sql

```
select
       count(*)
from
       sys.v_$session
where
       lockwait is not null;
```

Any non-zero number indicates a current blocking lock situation and can be investigated further by running this query:

```
select
       a.username blocked_user,
```

```
        b.username blocking_user,
        w.sid waiting_session,
        h.sid holding_session,
        w.type,
        decode(h.lmode,  1,'no lock',
                         2,'row share',
                         3,'row exclusive',
                 4,'share',
                 5,'share row exclusive',
                 6,'exclusive','none') lmode,
        decode(w.request, 1,'no lock',
                 2,'row share',
                 3,'row exclusive',
                 4,'share',
                 5,'share row exclusive',
                 6,'exclusive','none') request,
        a.row_wait_row# row_waited_on,
        w.id1,
        w.id2,
        w.ctime blocked_user_wait_secs,
        u1.name || '.' || t1.name locked_object
from
        sys.v_$lock w,
        sys.v_$lock h,
        sys.v_$session a,
        sys.v_$session b,
        sys.v_$locked_object o,
        sys.user$ u1,
        sys.obj$ t1
where
        h.lmode != 0 and
        w.request != 0 and
        w.type = h.type and
        w.id1 = h.id1 and
        w.id2 = h.id2 and
        b.sid = h.sid and
        a.sid = w.sid and
        h.sid = o.session_id and
        o.object_id = t1.obj# and
        u1.user# = t1.owner#
order by
        4,3;
```

Pinpointing Sessions with Problem SQL

Although this section mentions finding problem SQL and the sessions
that are making the problem SQL calls, the bulk of the coverage about
finding the most resource intensive SQL code that has run on a database
will be saved for the next chapter. The focus here is to pinpoint the
problem sessions that are currently issuing bad SQL calls rather than
create a historical analysis of the worst SQL issued on a system.

For example, if seeing the SQL currently running in a database session that has caused the most physical I/O is desired, a query like the *curriosql.sql* script would do the trick for Oracle 8i and above.

💾 curriosql.sql

```
select
        sid,
        username,
        sql_text
from
      sys.v_$sqltext a,
      sys.v_$session b
where
      b.sql_address = a.address
      and b.sid =
(select
      sid
from
(select
        b.sid sid,
        nvl(b.username,p.name) username,
        sum(value) total_user_io
from
      sys.v_$statname c,
      sys.v_$sesstat a,
      sys.v_$session b,
      sys.v_$bgprocess p
where
        a.statistic#=c.statistic# and
        p.paddr (+) = b.paddr and
        b.sid=a.sid and
        c.name in ('physical reads','physical writes',
                    'physical reads direct',
                    'physical reads direct (lob)',
                    'physical writes direct',
                    'physical writes direct (lob)')
group by
        b.sid,
        nvl(b.username,p.name)
order by
        3 desc)
where
        rownum < 2)
order by
        a.piece;
```

Output from such a query might look like this:

```
SID  USERNAME      SQL_TEXT
-----------------------------------------------------
19   ORA_MONITOR   SELECT COUNT(*) FROM ADMISSION
19   ORA_MONITOR   WHERE PATIENT_ID BETWEEN 1 AND 100;
```

Similar queries could be issued to uncover the SQL that the current memory or CPU is running as well. Of course, the previous query will give only the currently running SQL for a session, which may or may not be the code that has contributed to the session's resource consumption.

Some higher-level analysis can be done to answer questions like "What sessions have parsed Cartesian join statements?" by issuing the *cartsession.sql* script.

cartsession.sql

```
select
      username,
      count(distinct c.hash_value) nbr_stmts
from
    sys.v_$sql a,
    sys.dba_users b,
    sys.v_$sql_plan c
where
      a.parsing_user_id = b.user_id
      and    options = 'cartesian'
      and    operation like '%join%'
      and    a.hash_value = c.hash_value
group by
      username
order by
      2 desc;
```

Running this query on an Oracle 9i server may yield results similar to this:

```
USERNAME       NBR_STMTS
---------      ---------
ORA_USR1               2
SYSMAN                 2
ERADMIN                1
```

Once it has been determined that Cartesian joins have occurred on a system, look further and find the actual SQL statements themselves by using a query like the *cartsql.sql* script. Note again that this is only on Oracle 9i or above.

cartsql.sql

```
select
      *
from
```

```
      sys.v_$sql
where
      hash_value in
(select
      hash_value
from
      sys.v_$sql_plan
where
      options = 'CARTESIAN'
      and operation LIKE '%JOIN%' )
order by
      hash_value;
```

	SQL_TEXT	SHARABLE_MEM	PERSISTENT_MEM	RUNTIME_MEM	SORTS	LOADED_VERSIONS	OPEN_VERSIONS	USERS_OPENING
1	SELECT bc_hit_ratio, lib_cache_hit_ratio, dd_cache_hit_ratio, mem_sort_ratio, parse_execute_ratio, buffer_busy_wait_ratio, rollback_cont_ratio, latch_miss_ratio, parallel_query_busy_ratio, percent_shared_pool_free, problem_tablespaces, problem_objects,	834152	14836	135372	37	1	0	0
2	SELECT round(((total_space_perm + total_space_temp) - (total_free_space_perm + nvl(total_free_space_temp,0)))/1048576,2) total_used_space, ROUND((total_free_space_perm +	110462	3276	31412	0	1	0	0
3	Select owner, object_type,'' Result_Type, object_name from DBA_OBJECTS Where ((object_name like :oLike) or (object_name like :InName)) and (owner<>:owner) UNION Select allo_owner, Decode(allo.object_type,'VIEW', 'VIEW COLUMN', 'TABLE', 'TABLE COLUMN'), abc.table_name Result_Type, atc.column_name object_name from	448563	11796	226760	6	1	0	0
4	select username, 1 from DBA_USERS where username='SYS' union select role,2 from DBA_ROLES where role='DBA' union select name, 3 from	101560	3496	60056	3	1	0	0
5	SELECT 900, (total_space - total_free_space)/1048576 FROM (SELECT SUM(bytes) AS total_space FROM	79076	2388	22848	0	1	1	1
6	SELECT bc_hit_ratio, lib_cache_hit_ratio, dd_cache_hit_ratio, mem_sort_ratio, parse_execute_ratio, buffer_busy_wait_ratio, rollback_cont_ratio, latch_miss_ratio, parallel_query_busy_ratio, percent_shared_pool_free, problem_tablespaces, problem_objects,	835631	14836	135372	37	1	0	0
7	SELECT ((total_space_perm + total_space_temp) - (total_free_space_perm +	110811	3216	31176	0	1	0	0

Figure 6.4: *SQL Statements That Contain at Least One Cartesian Join*

The above script is quite valuable as Cartesian joins can cause unnecessary system workload and be difficult to spot in SQL queries with many join predicates.

While there is no way to totally prevent users from accessing the database in ways that are not desired, their resource privileges can be limited, problem access patterns can be uncovered, and excessive usage can be found by applying the techniques and scripts highlighted in this chapter. When doing so, the starting techniques of another very valuable form of performance analysis, termed workload analysis, will be applied.

Once the problem sessions are identified, then turn attention to finding and either removing or tuning the problem SQL calls that are causing any system slowdowns. This second set of workload analysis techniques will be covered in the next chapter.

Summary

This chapter showed how to use an analytic technique called workload analysis and also looked at session activity using a variety of analysis techniques and scripts. The main topics covered were finding storage hogs, i.e. how much space each user account has consumed, locating top resource sessions and pinpointing sessions with problem SQL. The next chapter will go into more detail concerning problem SQL and triage.

Troubleshooting Problem SQL and Triage

Troubleshooting Problem SQL

As a DBA, the right game plan needs to be in place for finding and fixing problem SQL code in the database. Fortunately, Oracle is better than most DBMSs at providing information in the data dictionary to help locate and analyze potentially bad SQL. By using the roadmap and scripts provided in this chapter, short work of pinpointing any bad SQL that is run though the system should be easy to accomplish.

What is Bad SQL?

Before problem SQL can be identified in the database, ask the question "What is bad SQL?" What criteria should be used when beginning the hunt for problem SQL in the critical systems?

Understand that even the seasoned experts disagree on what constitutes efficient and inefficient SQL, so there is no way to sufficiently answer this question to every Oracle professionals' satisfaction. What follows are some general criteria that can be used when evaluating the output from various database monitors or personal diagnostic scripts:

- Overall response (elapsed) time: This is how much time the query took to parse, execute, and fetch the data needed to satisfy the query. It should not include the network time needed to make the round trip from the requesting client workstation to the database server.

- CPU time: This is how much CPU time the query took to parse, execute, and fetch the data needed to satisfy the query.

- Physical I/O: Often used as the major statistic in terms of identifying good vs. bad SQL, this is a measure of how many disk reads the query caused to satisfy the user's request. While disk I/O should be controlled wherever possible, it is important that focus is not put solely on physical I/O as the single benchmark of inefficient SQL. Make no mistake, disk access is slower than memory access and also consumes processing time making the physical to logical transition, but look at the entire I/O picture of a SQL statement, which includes looking at a statement's logical I/O as well.

- Logical I/O: This is a measure of how many memory reads the query took to satisfy the user's request. The goal of tuning I/O for a query should be to examine both logical and physical I/O, and use appropriate mechanisms to keep both to a minimum.

- Repetition: This is a measure of how often the query has been executed. A problem in this area is not as easy to spot as the others unless one knows one's application well. A query that takes a fraction of a second to execute may still be causing a headache on the system if it is executed erroneously. For example, a query that executes in a runaway PL/SQL loop over and over again.

There are other criteria that can be examined like sort activity or access plan statistics that show items such as Cartesian joins and the like, but more often than not, these measures are reflected in the criteria listed above.

Fortunately, Oracle records all the above measures, which makes tracking the SQL that has been submitted against an Oracle database a lot easier.

Pinpointing Bad SQL

When looking for inefficient SQL in the library cache begins, start by defining what constitutes inefficient SQL. Remember, Oracle has two separate optimizer goals, each with different definitions of what it means to be best:

- First rows: Fetch the desired rows with a minimum amount of block touches (favors indexes).

- All rows: Fetch the desired rows using the least amount of computing resources (favors full scans).

Far and away, most Oracle systems will want to optimize their SQL using *first_rows* optimization, configuring the optimizer to use indexes to fetch results as quickly as possible, even if the index access means more computing resources.

Proactive SQL Troubleshooting

As has been noted, the best way to tune the database is by tuning the workload as a whole, examining historical SQL execution patterns. The easiest way to perform historical SQL analysis is to use STATSPACK or AWR, and set the SQL collection thresholds to capture exceptional SQL based on the DBA's own characteristics.

To find inefficient SQL in real-time, a good top SQL script to use for Oracle is the *topsql.sql* query. It will pull the top 20 SQL statements as determined initially by disk reads per execution, but the sort order can be changed to sort on logical I/O, elapsed time, and such:

💾 topsql.sql

```
select
        sql_text ,
        username ,
        disk_reads_per_exec,
        buffer_gets_per_exec,
        buffer_gets ,
        disk_reads,
        parse_calls ,
        sorts ,
        executions ,
        loads,
        rows_processed ,
        hit_ratio,
        first_load_time ,
        sharable_mem ,
        persistent_mem ,
```

```
        runtime_mem,
        cpu_time_secs,
        cpu_time_secs_per_execute,
        elapsed_time_secs,
        elapsed_time_secs_per_execute,
        address,
        hash_value
from
(select
        sql_text ,
        b.username ,
        round((a.disk_reads/
        decode(a.executions,0,1,a.executions)),2)
        disk_reads_per_exec,
        a.disk_reads ,
        a.buffer_gets ,
        round((a.buffer_gets/
        decode(a.executions,0,1,a.executions)),2)
        buffer_gets_per_exec,
        a.parse_calls ,
        a.sorts ,
        a.executions ,
        a.loads,
        a.rows_processed ,
        100 - round(100 *
        a.disk_reads/
        greatest(a.buffer_gets,1),2) hit_ratio,
        a.first_load_time ,
        sharable_mem ,
        persistent_mem ,
        runtime_mem,
        round(cpu_time / 1000000,3) cpu_time_secs,
        round((cpu_time / 1000000)/
        decode(a.executions,0,1,a.executions),3)
        cpu_time_secs_per_execute,
        round(elapsed_time / 1000000,3) elapsed_time_secs,
        round((elapsed_time /
        1000000)/decode(a.executions,0,1,a.executions),3)
        elapsed_time_secs_per_execute,
        address,
        hash_value
from
        sys.v_$sqlarea a,
        sys.all_users b
where
        a.parsing_user_id=b.user_id and
        b.username not in ('SYS','SYSTEM')
        order by 3 desc)
where
      rownum < 21;
```

Output from this query might resemble the following:

	SQL_TEXT	USERNAME	DISK_READS_PER_EXEC	BUFFER_GETS_PER_EXEC	BUFFER_GETS	DISK_READS	PARSE_CALLS	SORTS	EX
1	begin PERFCNTR_24x7_QUERIES.fetchcursor20_2(VAR1_	USR1	122.5	78886.5	157773	245	2	0	
2	SELECT 956, (INVALID_OBJECTS + UNUSABLE_INDEXES) AS TOTAL FROM (SELECT	USR1	94	45723.5	91447	188	1	0	
3	SELECT 'PERFCNTR_24x7_QUERIES', PERFCNTR_24x7_QUERIES.GetVersion from DUAL UNION	USR1	67	975	975	67	1	1	
4	SELECT 900, (total_space - total_free_space)/1048576 FROM (SELECT SUM(bytes) AS total_space FROM	USR1	18.5	238	476	37	1	0	
5	select 99 /100, 1 - to_number(to_char(to_date('1997-11-0	USR1	11	86	86	11	1	0	
6	SELECT 955, COUNT(*) FROM SYS.DBA_TABLES WHER	USR1	5.5	30784	61568	11	1	0	
7	SELECT 998, COUNT(*) FROM (SELECT USERNAME FROM SYS.DBA_USERS WHERE	USR1	3.5	239.5	479	7	1	16	
8	select a.machine, b.count from (SELECT DISTINCT MACHINE FROM V$SESSION WHERE TYPE =	USR1	3	63	63	3	1	1	
9	SELECT 977, a.active active_jobs,b.due-a.active jobs_waiting,c.snp_processes - a.active idle_jobs,c.snp_processes total_jobs FROM (SELECT	USR1	2.5	70.5	141	5	1	2	
10	begin PERFCNTR_24x7_QUERIES.fetchcursor22_5(VAR1_	USR1	2.5	70.5	141	5	2	0	
11	begin PERFCNTR_24x7_QUERIES.fetchcursor16_3(VAR1_	USR1	1.67	114.5	687	10	6	0	
12	SELECT 948, ACTIVE_COUNT,ROUND(100 * (ACTIVE_COUNT / TOTAL_COUNT),2) AS ACTIVE_PCT	USR1	1.67	76.17	457	10	1	0	
13	begin PERFCNTR_24x7_QUERIES.fetchcursor1_2(VAR1_	USR1	1.33	156.17	937	8	6	0	
14	begin PERFCNTR_24x7_QUERIES.fetchcursor3_3(VAR1_	USR1	.83	107.83	647	5	6	0	

Figure 7.1: *Output From the Top 20 SQL Query*

It is important to examine the output of this query and see how it uses the criteria set forth at the beginning of this chapter to pinpoint problematic SQL.

First, start by looking at Figure 7.2 and focus on the circled columns.

	PERSISTENT_MEM	RUNTIME_MEM	CPU_TIME_SECS	CPU_TIME_SECS_PER_EXECUTE	ELAPSED_TIME_SECS	ELAPSED_TIME_SECS_PER_EXECUTE	ADDRESS	HASH_VALUE
1	540	276	1.642	.821	4.814	2.407	672621C0	3077230681
2	696	30300	.521	.26	1.204	.602	6746A26C	2965734772
3	1400	3684	.11	.11	.399	.399	674D57CC	2741343822
4	2388	22848	.06	.03	1.368	.684	6746A848	3829441909
5	700	876	.02	.02	.079	.079	674FA28C	1276527007
6	660	12748	.26	.13	.293	.147	6746A460	2911359602
7	692	100596	.05	.025	.07	.035	67469D84	3547812303
8	664	4036	.02	.02	.034	.034	674F4504	2966647892
9	852	4388	.02	.01	.054	.027	674688A0	482951707

Figure 7.2: *Output From the Top 20 SQL Query That Shows Timing Statistics*

The output displays both CPU and elapsed times for each SQL query. The times are shown both cumulatively in seconds and per execution indicating, for example, that the first query in the result set has accumulated almost five seconds of total execution time and runs for about two and half seconds each time it is executed. The query to sort by any of these timed statistics can be changed depending on the criteria needed to bubble the worst running SQL to the top of the result set.

Again, sadly, these metrics are lost when any database version under Oracle 9i is used.

Looking back at Figure 7.2, the columns can be seen that will help with examining the I/O characteristics of each SQL statement. The number of disk reads (physical I/O) and buffer gets (logical I/O) are shown along with numbers that display the average I/O consumption of each SQL statement.

Watch out for single execution SQL!

Queries that have only been executed once may have misleading statistics with respect to disk reads as the data needed for the first run of the query was likely read in from disk to memory.

Therefore, the number of disk reads per execution should drop for subsequent executions and the hit ratio should rise.

The executions column of the top SQL's result set will provide clues to the repetition metric for the query. When troubleshooting a slow system, be on the lookout for any query that shows an execution count that is significantly larger than any other query on the system. It may be that the query is in an inefficient PL/SQL loop or other problematic programming construct. Only by bringing the query to the attention of the application developers will one know if the query is being mishandled from a programming standpoint.

Once the SQL statements are found through Oracle's diagnostic views, get the entire SQL text for the statements that appear inefficient. Note the *hash_value* values for each SQL statement, and then issue the *fullsql.sql* script to obtain the full SQL statement:

🖫 **fullsql.sql**

```
select
    sql_text
from
```

```
        sys.v_$sqltext
where
        hash_value = <enter hash value for sql statement>
order by
        piece;
```

One of the first activities in Oracle troubleshooting is to quickly check to see what SQL is currently executing to understand if any resource-intensive SQL is dragging down the database's overall performance levels. This is very easy to do and only involves making one change to the already discussed *topsql.sql* query. Add the following filter to the main query's WHERE clause:

```
where
        a.parsing_user_id=b.user_id and
        b.username not in ('SYS','SYSTEM') and
        a.users_executing > 0
order by
        3 desc;
```

This query change will display the worst SQL that is currently running in the database so one can quickly tell if any queries are to blame for a dip in database performance.

Tricks for SQL Troubleshooting

The troubleshooting techniques that have been shown so far are traditional ways of pinpointing problem SQL in Oracle. However, there are some new methods that can be used to get a handle on how well the SQL in the database is executing. For example, the question of how many total SQL statements are causing Cartesian joins on the system may need to be answered. The following *cartcount.sql* query can find all Cartesian joins:

🖫 cartcount.sql

```
select
        count(distinct hash_value) carteisan_statements,
        count(*) total_cartesian_joins
from
        sys.v_$sql_plan
where
        options = 'CARTESIAN' and
        operation like '%JOIN%';
```

Output from this query might resemble the following. Note that it is possible for a single SQL statement to contain more than one Cartesian join:

```
CARTESIAN_STATEMENTS      TOTAL_CARTESIAN_JOINS
-------------------       ---------------------
                4                             6
```

Then view the actual SQL statements containing the Cartesian joins along with their performance metrics by using the *cartsql.sql* query:

cartsql.sql

```
select
        *
from
        sys.v_$sql
where
        hash_value in
(select
        hash_value
 from
        sys.v_$sql_plan
 where
        options = 'CARTESIAN'
 AND    operation LIKE '%JOIN%' )
order by hash_value;
```

Another big area of interest is monitoring table scan activity. Most DBAs do not worry about small-table scans since Oracle can often access small tables more efficiently through a full scan than through index access; the small table is just cached and accessed. Large-table scans, however, are another matter. While large-table full-table scans are sometimes justified, i.e. reading the majority of blocks in the table, they also indicate missing indexes or suboptimal SQL optimization. Most DBAs in OLTP environments will remove all large-table full scans with smart index placement or intelligent partitioning. Using the *v$sql_plan* view, it is easy to quickly identify any SQL statement that contains one or more large-table scans, and even 'large' can be defined in one's own terms.

The following *tabscan.sql* query shows any SQL statement that contains a large-table scan, defined in this query as a table over 1MB, along with a

count of how many large scans it causes for each execution, the total
number of times the statement has been executed, and then the sum
total of all scans it has caused on the system:

💾 **tabscan.sql**

```
select
        sql_text,
        total_large_scans,
        executions,
        executions * total_large_scans sum_large_scans
from
(select
        sql_text,
        count(*) total_large_scans,
        executions
from
        sys.v_$sql_plan a,
        sys.dba_segments b,
        sys.v_$sql c
where
        a.object_owner (+) = b.owner
and     a.object_name (+) = b.segment_name
and     b.segment_type in ('TABLE', 'TABLE PARTITION')
and     a.operation like '%TABLE%'
and     a.options = 'FULL'
and     c.hash_value = a.hash_value
and     b.bytes / 1024 > 1024
group by
        sql_text, executions)
order by
        4 desc;
```

	SQL_TEXT	TOTAL_LARGE_SCANS	EXECUTIONS	SUM_LARGE_SCANS
1	select o.owner#,o.obj#,decode(o.linkname,null, decode(u.name,null,'SYS',u.name),o.remoteowner),	1	19	19
2	SELECT 1 FROM SYS.DBA_OBJECTS WHERE ROWNUM = 1 MINUS SELECT 1 FROM SYS.DBA_EXTENTS WHERE ROWNUM = 1 MINUS	2	2	4
3	SELECT 1 FROM SYS.DBA_OBJECTS WHERE ROWNUM = 1 MINUS SELECT 1 FROM SYS.DBA_EXTENTS WHERE ROWNUM = 1 MINUS	2	1	2
4	SELECT OWNER,TABLE_NAME,NUM_ROWS,PCT_FREE,PCT_USED,TA	1	2	2
5	EXPLAIN PLAN SET STATEMENT_ID='10118429' INTO EMBARCADERO	1	1	1
6	SELECT OWNER,TABLE_NAME,NUM_ROWS,PCT_FREE,PCT_USED,TABLESPA	1	1	1
7	select count(*) from eradmin.emp	1	1	1
8	select distinct i.obj# from sys.idl_ub1$ i where i.obj#>=:1 and i.obj# not	1	1	1

Figure 7.3: *Output Showing Large-table Scan Activity from an Oracle 9i Database*

This query provides important output and poses a number of interesting
questions. As a DBA, should more worrying be done about a SQL

statement that causes only one large-table scan, but has been executed 1,000 times, or a SQL statement that has ten large scans in it, but has only been executed a handful of times? Every Oracle tuning professional will likely have an opinion on this, but regardless, it can be seen how such a query can assist with identifying SQL statements that have the potential to cause system slowdowns.

Oracle 9.2 has introduced another new performance view, *v$sql_plan_statistics* , that can be used to get even more statistical data regarding the execution of inefficient SQL statements. This view can tell how many buffer gets, disk reads and such that each step in a SQL execution plan caused, and even goes so far as to list the cumulative and last executed counts of all held metrics.

This view can be referenced to get a great perspective of which step in a SQL execution plan is really responsible for most of the resource consumption. Note that to enable the collection of data for this view, the Oracle configuration parameter *statistics_level* must be set to ALL.

An example that utilizes this view is the following *planstats.sql* script that shows the statistics for one problem SQL statement:

🖫 planstats.sql

```
select
        operation,
        options,
        object_owner,
        object_name,
        executions,
        last_output_rows,
        last_cr_buffer_gets,
        last_cu_buffer_gets,
        last_disk_reads,
        last_disk_writes,
        last_elapsed_time
from
        sys.v_$sql_plan a,
        sys.v_$sql_plan_statistics b
where
        a.hash_value = b.hash_value and
        a.id = b.operation_id and
        a.hash_value = <enter hash value>
order by a.id;
```

	OPERATION	OPTIONS	OBJECT_OWNER	OBJECT_NAME	EXECUTIONS	LAST_OUTPUT_ROWS	LAST_CR_BUFFER_GETS	LAST_CU_BUFFER_GETS	LAST_DISK_READS	LAST
1	MERGE JOIN	CARTESIAN	[NULL]	[NULL]	1	31849	46	0	18	
2	TABLE ACCESS	FULL	ERADMIN	PATIENT	1	22	24	0	5	
3	BUFFER	SORT	[NULL]	[NULL]	1	31849	22	0	13	
4	PARTITION RANGE	ALL	[NULL]	[NULL]	1	1507	22	0	13	
5	TABLE ACCESS	FULL	ERADMIN	ADMISSION	1	1507	22	0	13	

Figure 7.4: *Example Output Showing Statistical Metrics for Each Step in a Query Execution Plan*

Understanding the current state an shape of the objects being used in the queries needing to be tuned can unlock clues about how the SQL code might need to be restructured. For example, it may be realized that critical foreign keys that are used over and over again in various sets of join operations have not been indexed, or that a million-row table is found to be a perfect candidate for a bitmap index given the current *where* predicate.

Object-based solutions are another option for SQL tuning analysts. This route involves things like intelligent index creation, partitioning, and more. In order to do this, first find the objects that will benefit from such modification, which in turn will enhance the overall runtime performance.

For example, if the choice is made to investigate better use of partitioning, the first thing is to locate large tables that are the consistent targets of full-table scans. The *tabscan.sql* query below will identify the actual objects that are the target of such scans. It displays the table owner, table name, the table type (standard, partitioned), the table size in KB, the number of SQL statements that cause a scan to be performed, the number of total scans for the table each time the statement is executed, the number of SQL executions to date, and the total number of scans that the table has experienced (total single scans * executions):

🖫 **tabscan.sql**

```
select
    table_owner,
    table_name,
    table_type,
    size_kb,
```

```
      statement_count,
      reference_count,
      executions,
      executions * reference_count total_scans
from
   (select
   a.object_owner table_owner,
   a.object_name table_name,
   b.segment_type table_type,
   b.bytes / 1024 size_kb,
   sum(c.executions ) executions,
   count( distinct a.hash_value ) statement_count,
   count( * ) reference_count
from
    sys.v_$sql_plan a,
    sys.dba_segments b,
    sys.v_$sql c
where
    a.object_owner (+) = b.owner
    and a.object_name (+) = b.segment_name
    and b.segment_type in ('TABLE', 'TABLE PARTITION')
    and a.operation like '%TABLE%'
    and a.options = 'FULL'
    and a.hash_value = c.hash_value
    and b.bytes / 1024 > 1024
group by
    a.object_owner, a.object_name, a.operation,
    b.bytes / 1024, b.segment_type
order by
    4 desc, 1, 2 );
```

	TABLE_OWNER	TABLE_NAME	TABLE_TYPE	SIZE_KB	STATEMENT_COUNT	REFERENCE_COUNT	EXECUTIONS	TOTAL_SCANS
1	ERADMIN	EMP	TABLE	19456	2	2	2	4
2	ERADMIN	PATIENT	TABLE	3496	1	1	1	1
3	ERADMIN	ADMISSION	TABLE	3136	4	7	31	217

Figure 7.5: *Identifying Tables or Table Partitions That Have Been Scanned in Oracle*

The above query will help determine what tables might benefit from better indexing or partitioning. When reviewing such output, the question might arise that if the tables being scanned have indexes, why are the queries that are scanning the tables not making use of them?

While only examination of the actual SQL statements can answer the second part of that question, the first part can be answered through the following *unused_indx.sql* query:

🖫 unused_indx.sql

```
select distinct
    a.object_owner table_owner,
    a.object_name table_name,
    b.segment_type table_type,
    b.bytes / 1024 size_kb,
    d.index_name
from
    sys.v_$sql_plan a,
    sys.dba_segments b,
    sys.dba_indexes d
where
    a.object_owner (+) = b.owner
    and a.object_name (+) = b.segment_name
    and b.segment_type in ('TABLE', 'TABLE PARTITION')
    and a.operation like '%TABLE%'
    and a.options = 'FULL'
    and b.bytes / 1024 > 1024
    and b.segment_name = d.table_name
    and b.owner = d.table_owner
order by
    1, 2;
```

	TABLE_OWNER	TABLE_NAME	TABLE_TYPE	SIZE_KB	INDEX_NAME
1	ERADMIN	ADMISSION	TABLE	2048	I_ADMISSION1
2	ERADMIN	ADMISSION	TABLE	2048	I_ADMISSION2
3	ERADMIN	PATIENT	TABLE	3072	I_PATIENT1
4	ERADMIN	PATIENT	TABLE	3072	I_PATIENT2
5	ERADMIN	PATIENT	TABLE	3072	I_PATIENT3

Figure 7.6: *Output Showing Unused Indexes for Tables Being Scanned*

Such a query can create a mini unused indexes report that can be used to ensure that any large tables being scanned on the system have the proper indexing scheme.

Troubleshooting Triage

To optimally cache the working set of frequently accessed data, the data buffers can be monitored for short periods of time. An experienced DBA can measure the buffer efficiency with either the Automated Workload Repository (AWR) or STATSPACK with the script below. An overall system-wide data buffer hit ratio is not much help.

The following scripts can be used to get an idea of what is happening currently in the database. It prompts the user for a wait period, takes two STATSPACK snapshots and then does a quick time period summary of database changes. This is just a quick overview of SGA tuning. Other Rampant books provide significantly more detail on the subject.

Before revealing the script, the following is a sample of the output:

```
************************************************************
This will identify any single file whose read I/O
is more than 10% of the total read I/O of the database.

************************************************************


MYDATE            FILE_NAME                                   READS
---------------   -----------------------------------------   ---------
2000-12-20 11     /u03/oradata/PROD/pod01.dbf                 1,766

************************************************************
When the data buffer hit ratio falls below 90%, you
should consider adding to the db_block_buffer init.ora parameter

************************************************************


MYDATE            phys_writes BUFFER HIT RATIO
---------------   ----------- ----------------
20 Dec 11:23:47       101,888               91


************************************************************
When there are high disk sorts, you should investigate
increasing sort_area_size, or adding indexes to force index_full scans
************************************************************


MYDATE            SORTS_MEMORY  SORTS_DISK       RATIO
---------------   ------------ ------------ ---------------
20 Dec 11:23:47            109            1  .0091743119266


************************************************************
Buffer busy wait most frequently signal incorrectly configured database
writer (DBWR) or freelist cointention. This event means simply that another
session has the buffer pinned and that the session recording this event must
wait.

************************************************************


MYDATE            BUFFER_BUSY_WAIT
---------------   ----------------
```

```
20 Dec 11:23:47                    20

***************************************************************
Table fetch continued row indicates chained rows, or fetches of
long datatypes (long raw, blob)

Investigate increasing db_block_size or reorganizing tables
with chained rows.
***************************************************************


MYDATE             TABLE_FETCH_CONTINUED_ROW
---------------    -------------------------
20 Dec 11:23:47                        1,551


***************************************************************
Long-table full table scans might indicate a need to:

- Make the offending tables parallel query
(alter table xxx parallel degree yyy;)
- Place the table in the RECYCLE pool
- Build an index on the table to remove the FTS

***************************************************************


MYDATE             FTS
---------------    ------------
20 Dec 11:23:47         148
```

The listing above shows the significant value of this report. A time-series report of Oracle behavior can be seen and the time interval gets to be chosen. An experienced DBA would likely run the following *quick.ksh* script using a five-minute time interval.

💾 quick.ksh (partial)

```
awr_quick.ksh


spool rpt_last.lst

set pages 9999;
set feedback on;
set verify off;

column reads  format 999,999,999
column writes format 999,999,999

select
   to_char(sn.end_interval_time,'yyyy-mm-dd HH24'),
   (newreads.value-oldreads.value) reads,
   (newwrites.value-oldwrites.value) writes
from
```

```
      dba_hist_sysstat oldreads,
      dba_hist_sysstat newreads,
      dba_hist_sysstat oldwrites,
      dba_hist_sysstat newwrites,
      dba_hist_snapshot    sn
where
      newreads.snap_id = (select max(sn.snap_id)
from dba_hist_snapshot)
      and newwrites.snap_id = (select max(sn.snap_id)
from dba_hist_snapshot)
      and oldreads.snap_id = sn.snap_id-1
      and oldwrites.snap_id = sn.snap_id-1
      and oldreads.stat_name = 'physical reads'
      and newreads.stat_name = 'physical reads'
      and oldwrites.stat_name = 'physical writes'
      and newwrites.stat_name = 'physical writes'
;

prompt ************************************************************
prompt  This will identify any single file who's read I/O
prompt  is more than 10% of the total read I/O of the database.
prompt
prompt  The "hot" file should be examined, and the hot table/index
prompt  should be identified using STATSPACK.
prompt
prompt  - The busy file should be placed on a disk device with
prompt    "less busy" files to minimize read delay and channel
prompt    contention.
prompt
prompt  - If small file has a hot small table, place the table
prompt    in the KEEP pool
prompt
prompt  - If the file has a large-table full-table scan, place
prompt    the table in the RECYCLE pool and turn on parallel query
prompt    for the table.
prompt ************************************************************

column mydate format a16
column file_name format a40
column reads  format 999,999,999

select
   to_char(sn.end_interval_time,'yyyy-mm-dd HH24')  mydate,
   new.filename                         file_name,
   new.phyrds-old.phyrds                reads
from
   dba_hist_filestatxs old,   dba_hist_filestatxs new,   dba_hist_snapshot
snwhere   sn.snap_id = (select max(snap_id) from dba_hist_snapshot) and
new.snap_id = sn.snap_id
and
   old.snap_id = sn.snap_id-1
and
   new.filename = old.filename
--and
--   new.phyrds-old.phyrds > 10000
and
   (new.phyrds-old.phyrds)*10 >
(
select
```

```
       (newreads.value-oldreads.value) reads
from
   dba_hist_sysstat oldreads,
   dba_hist_sysstat newreads,
   dba_hist_snapshot    sn1
where
   sn.snap_id = sn1.snap_id
and newreads.snap_id = sn.snap_id
and oldreads.snap_id = sn.snap_id-1
and oldreads.stat_name = 'physical reads'
and newreads.stat_name = 'physical reads'
and (newreads.value-oldreads.value) > 0)
;

prompt ***********************************************************
prompt  This will identify any single file who's write I/O
prompt  is more than 10% of the total write I/O of the database.
prompt
prompt  The "hot" file should be examined, and the hot table/index
prompt  should be identified using STATSPACK.
prompt
prompt  - The busy file should be placed on a disk device with
prompt    "less busy" files to minimize write delay and channel
prompt    channel contention.
prompt
prompt  - If small file has a hot small table, place the table
prompt    in the KEEP pool
prompt
prompt ***********************************************************
```

Summary

Fixing problem SQL has been the focus of this chapter. A definition of what qualifies as bad SQL has been given with some basic criteria for identification and how to troubleshoot databases by using queries to examine tables.

Now that the basic methods for troubleshooting SQL have been covered, move on and look at the extra cost Active Session History (ASH) tables.

Troubleshooting ASH

8

Using Active Session History (ASH) for Troubleshooting

Prior to Oracle 10g, capturing wait event information was a cumbersome process involving the setting of special events, e.g. 10046, and the reading of complex trace dumps. Fortunately, Oracle 10g has simplified the way that wait event information is captured and there are a wealth of new *v$* and *wrh$* views relating to Oracle wait events.

Check the license!

Extra-cost Oracle Diagnostic Pack must be purchased to view the ASH tables. While nothing prevents querying these tables, the access is audited.

Oracle has already developed a great data collection infrastructure within the Automated Workload Repository (AWR) which is built into the Oracle kernel. AWR snapshots will rarely impose any measurable system load and by default, Oracle collects AWR data in hourly snapshots for long periods of time that are determined by the DBA.

To complement AWR, Oracle has created the Automated Session History data collection mechanism which keeps highly detailed session information for a short period of time, usually an hour or 30 minutes, as specified by the DBA.

Within the Oracle core software, Oracle Corporation balances the issue of statistics detail and overall system performance with AWR (long-term proactive) vs. ASH (short-term reactive). Oracle's own monitoring and statistics collection mechanisms, STATSPACK and AWR, are built to be very unobtrusive because they quickly extract snapshots of accumulators from the *x$* fixed tables. Oracle now offers wait event statistics on more than 800 specific wait events. These wait events are the result of Oracle breaking out their latch waits into their individual components and breaking-out enqueue waits (locks) into a finer level of granularity.

The foundation concept of the ASH architecture is called the time model, and Oracle 10g has introduced several important new wait event *v$* views.

V$ View	DBA_HIST View
v$active_sess_hist	dba_hist_active_sess_history
v$sys_time_model	dba_hist_sys_time_model
v$active_session_history	dba_hist_active_sess_history
v$event_histogram	No equivalent DBA view

Table 8.1: *V$Views and DBA_Hist Views*

Unlike the old-fashioned *v$session* and *v$session_wait* views where waits can only be seen at the exact instant when they occurred, the new *v$session_wait_history* and *v$sys_time_model* views allow Oracle to capture system waits details in a time-series mode. One of the most important areas of Oracle 10g wait event tuning is the Oracle 10g Active Session History (ASH). ASH data is visualized through the *v$active_sess_hist* view and the *wrh$active_session_history* tables.

Collecting ASH Wait Information

The ASH tables can be used for both real time and historical trend analysis, but the real value is in time-series trend analysis. However, ASH views such as *v$active_session_history* and *v$session_wait_history* only report sessions' histories for a short, sliding period of time in a SGA buffer.

The *v$* views are good for real-time monitoring using OEM, but they are not very good for showing wait-related performance trends over a long time interval.

The AWR that holds ASH history is sampled every second and stored inside *x$* structures that are materialized by the *v$active_session_history* and *v$session_wait_history* views and stored inside a circular SGA buffer. When an AWR snapshot is taken, only the current session wait information that exists at that precise moment is transferred from the *v$active_session_history* in-memory view into the persistent *dba_hist_active_sess_history* table.

The default collection retention for AWR data is only seven days, but the retention period can be increased by using the new dbms package called *dbms_workload_repository.modify_snapshot_settings*. It is a good idea to increase the storage of detail information over longer time periods.

Once transferred to AWR tables, the data can be used for longer periods of time and the length of these time periods can be adjusted by the DBA as needed. In order to track historical data longer than a few minutes or seconds in earlier Oracle versions, the DBA would have to increase the retention period for the ASH tables. This will change the retention period and collection frequency, thereby providing users with longer time periods of data:

```
begin
  dbms_workload_repository. modify_snapshot_settings (
    retention => 43200,        -- Minutes (= 30 Days).
    interval  => 30);          -- Minutes.
END;
/
```

In the above script, the retention period is indicated as 30 days (43200 min) while the interval between each snapshot is 30 minutes. Changes to these settings will be apparent if the *dba_hist_wr_control* view is queried after this procedure is executed. Typically, the retention period should capture at least one complete workload cycle for the database. Some databases have hourly cycles, daily cycles and monthly processing cycles.

The retention argument of the *dbms_workload_repository.modify_snapshot_settings* procedure specifies how long all of the AWR data is retained, and many shops will keep at least two calendar years in order to capture repeating monthly workload cycles.

For wait event troubleshooting, the *interval* parameter is the most important. If the interval is longer than the amount of real-time session wait information stored in the circular buffer for the *v$active_session_history* and *v$session_wait_history* views, some wait session data will be lost. Another new innovation is the ability to use the Oracle 10g hash key for tracking session identification. This hash key allows the tracking of common session processes and allows inter-cal session tracking in cases like OCI session 'bouncing', where each call to Oracle is a different session ID.

The ASH samples for wait events every second and tracks the waits in the new *v$active_sess_hist* view. New data values are written to the *wrh$* tables every hour or when a new AWR snapshot is taken. The following are the Oracle *wrh$* wait event tables:

- *wrh$_active_session_history*
- *wrh$_active_session_history_bl*
- *wrh$_bg_event_summary*
- *wrh$_event_name*
- *wrh$_metric_name*
- *wrh$_sessmetric_history*
- *wrh$_sys_time_model*
- *wrh$_sys_time_model_bl*
- *wrh$_sysmetric_history*
- *wrh$_sysmetric_summary*
- *wrh$_sysstat*

- *wrh$_sysstat_bl*

- *wrh$_system_event*

- *wrh$_system_event_bl*

- *wrh$_waitclassmetric_history*

- *wrh$_waitstat*

- *wrh$_waitstat_bl*

The next section will detail the Oracle *dba_hist* views that are used to create time-series performance reports, both manually and within Oracle Enterprise Manager (OEM). The information will start with an overview of the *dba_hist* views and move on to examples of custom Oracle performance exception reports that can be easily generated from these views with SQL*Plus.

Using ASH for Troubleshooting

At a basic level, the ASH stores the history of a recent session's activity and facilitates the analysis of the system performance at the current time. The ASH is designed as a rolling buffer in memory, and earlier information is overwritten when needed. The ASH uses the memory of the SGA. Oracle keeps session history in the circular memory buffer in the SGA. This means that the greater the database activity is, the smaller the amount of time session history available in the ASH view is.

For long-term retention, there is the *dba_hist_active_sess_history* view which stores the ASH history. However, *dba_hist_active_sess_history* is highly transient with sessions coming and going constantly. Remember, AWR only stores ASH data snapshots when an AWR snapshot is taken.

Once the AWR table data and inter-table relationships between AWR and performance metrics have been explained thoroughly, it will be important to understand how the *wrh$* tables are used as input to the Automatic Memory Manager (AMM), the Automatic Database Diagnostic Monitor (ADDM), and the SQL Tuning Advisor.

The creation of the AWR and the ASH provides a complete repository for diagnosing and fixing any Oracle performance issue. The AWR provides the foundation for sophisticated performance analysis including exception reporting, trend analysis, correlation analysis, hypothesis testing and data mining. A good place to start is with time-series wait event analysis using the Oracle ASH tables.

Oracle's Graham Wood, inventor of ASH, notes in his presentation titled *Sifting through the ASHes: Performance Analysis with the Oracle 10g Active Session History*:

"Internally, Oracle stores ASH data in ASH RAM buffers within the shared pool before writing the data to the ASH data files."

```
select
 * from v$sgastat where name like 'ASH buffers';

POOL         NAME                        BYTES
------------ --------------------------- ----------
shared pool  ASH buffers                  65011712
```

The ASH samples every 10 seconds and then writes every one of ten samples to the *dba_hist_active_sess_history* table.

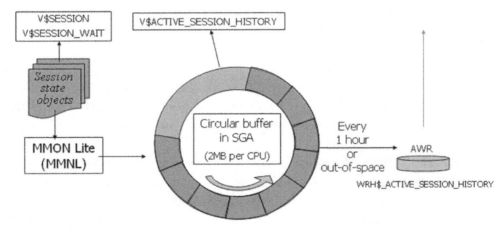

Figure 8.1: *Oracle's ASH Process*

This collection process allows the DBA to answer many important tuning questions:

- Where is time being spent?

- What events were taking the most time?

- What was a session doing?

- What does a SQL statement wait for?

ASH reports on active, non-idle sessions such as sessions waiting on a non-idle event, and this might be a small portion of the Oracle sessions. The design goal of ASH is to hold one hour of activity information in memory. The ASH component keeps this data:

- Wait event detail

- Session details

- SQL details such as the execution plan and step costs

- Tables and indexes like *Object#*, *File#*, and *Block#*

- Application information such as *program, module, action*, and *client_id*

Tip - Dumping ASH Data to a Flat File

The following commands are designed to dump the ASH data to a flat file. This is useful for analyzing transaction waits at a super-detailed level:

```
SQL>oradebug setmypid

SQL>oradebug dump ashdump 10

SQL>alter session set events 'immediate trace name ashdump level 10';
```

Figure 8.2 shows the relationships between the ASH structures.

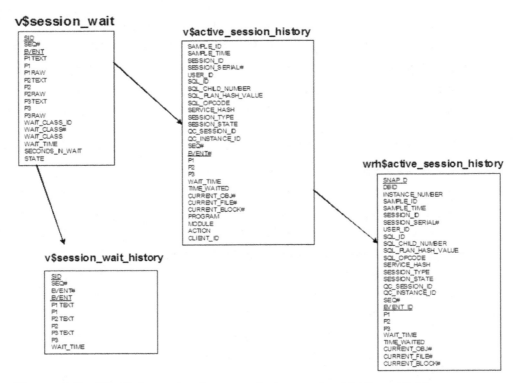

v$session_wait

SID
SEQ#
EVENT
P1 TEXT
P1
P1 RAW
P2 TEXT
P2
P2 RAW
P3 TEXT
P3
P3 RAW
WAIT_CLASS_ID
WAIT_CLASS#
WAIT_CLASS
WAIT_TIME
SECONDS_IN_WAIT
STATE

v$active_session_history

SAMPLE_ID
SAMPLE_TIME
SESSION_ID
SESSION_SERIAL#
USER_ID
SQL_ID
SQL_CHILD_NUMBER
SQL_PLAN_HASH_VALUE
SQL_OPCODE
SERVICE_HASH
SESSION_TYPE
SESSION_STATE
QC_SESSION_ID
QC_INSTANCE_ID
SEQ#
EVENT#
P1
P2
P3
WAIT_TIME
TIME_WAITED
CURRENT_OBJ#
CURRENT_FILE#
CURRENT_BLOCK#
PROGRAM
MODULE
ACTION
CLIENT_ID

wrh$active_session_history

SNAP_ID
DBID
INSTANCE_NUMBER
SAMPLE_ID
SAMPLE_TIME
SESSION_ID
SESSION_SERIAL#
USER_ID
SQL_ID
SQL_CHILD_NUMBER
SQL_PLAN_HASH_VALUE
SQL_OPCODE
SERVICE_HASH
SESSION_TYPE
SESSION_STATE
QC_SESSION_ID
QC_INSTANCE_ID
SEQ#
EVENT_ID
P1
P2
P3
WAIT_TIME
TIME_WAITED
CURRENT_OBJ#
CURRENT_FILE#
CURRENT_BLOCK#

v$session_wait_history

SID
SEQ#
EVENT#
EVENT
P1 TEXT
P1
P2 TEXT
P2
P3 TEXT
P3
WAIT_TIME

Figure 8.2: *The Relationship Between v$ views and wrh$ Event Tables*

It will be useful to look at examples of how the *v$session_event* view might be used in real life. In this example, end users have started complaining that they recently started to experience large delays when running a production application.

In some ERP applications like Oracle Applications and SAP, a single user account is used to connect to the database. In these cases, the DBA can issue the following statement to determine the particular event application for which the sessions are waiting:

💾 **session_waits.sql**

```
select
   se.event,
   sum(se.total_waits),
   sum(se.total_timeouts),
   sum(se.time_waited/100) time_waited
```

```
from
   v$session_event se,
   v$session      sess
where
   sess.username = 'SAPR3'
and
   sess.sid = se.sid
group by
   se.event
order by 2 DESC;
```

The output of this script might look like the following:

```
                 Waits for user SAPR3

                             SUM    SUM          TIME
EVENT                        WAITS  TIMEOUTS     WAITED
-------------------------    -----  ---------    ------
SQL*Net message to client    7,824  0               .06
SQL*Net message from client  7,812  0        312,969.73
db file sequential read      3,199  0             16.23
SQL*Net more data to client    590  0               .08
SQL*Net break/reset to client  418  0                .2
direct path read               328  0               .01
SQL*Net more data from client   78  0              3.29
latch free                      62  10              .08
db file scattered read          56  0               .75
log file sync                   47  0               .96
direct path write               32  0                .4
file open                       32  0                 0
library cache pin               13  0                 0
log file switch completion       3  0               .53
```

From the listing above, it can be concluded that end users spend most of their wait time waiting on the event SQL*Net message from client. This may indicate that there is some network-related issue causing clients too much wait time to send data to the database server.

Inside *v$active_session_history*

Oracle 10g first introduced the *v$active_session_history* view that keeps a history for recent active sessions' activity. Oracle takes snapshots of active database sessions every second without placing serious overhead on the system. A database session is considered active by Oracle when it is consuming CPU time or waiting for an event that does not belong to the idle wait class.

This view contains a considerable amount of information that is available in the *v$session* view, but it also has the *sample_time* column that points to a time in the past when a session was doing some work or waiting for a resource. The *v$active_session_history* view contains a single row for each session when sampling was performed.

The next query against the *dba_hist_active_sess_history* view reports a list of resources that were in high demand in the last hour. This query does not reflect idle wait events.

```
select
    e.name                          "Wait Event",
    SUM(h.wait_time + h.time_waited ) "Total Wait Time"
from
    v$active_session_history        h,
    v$event_name                    e
where
    h.event_id = e.event_id
and
    e.wait_class <> 'Idle'
group by
    e.name
order by
    2 DESC;
```

This query produces a listing like the one below, showing aggregate wait time for each event:

```
Wait Event                          Total Wait Time
------------------------------      ---------------
log buffer space                         9,638,484
db file sequential read                  8,442,918
log file switch completion               5,231,711
write complete waits                     5,200,368
db file scattered read                   4452,153
process startup                          3623,464
rdbms ipc reply                            917,765
log file sync                              662,224
latch free                                 550,241
latch: library cache                       370,696
db file parallel write                     364,641
free buffer waits                          319,151
latch: redo allocation                      64,984
LGWR wait for redo copy                     63,647
read by other session                       52,757
log file sequential read                    46,126
null event                                  33,011
log file parallel write                     26,280
SQL*Net E "SQL*Net" more data to client      8,894
latch: cache buffers chains                  7,005
```

```
control file sequential read            3,966
direct path read temp                      395
direct path write temp                     229
SQL*Net E "SQL*Net"  message to client      74
```

From the listing above, it can be seen that there is an issue with the *log buffer space* wait event that may indicate the need to increase the *log_buffer* parameter to increase the cache in order to minimize this possible bottleneck.

Using the AWR ASH view, a list of database users can be retrieved who have experienced high wait times during the time period between any two snapshots. The following query can be used to identify these target users:

< ash_user_wait_time.sql

```
select
   s.sid,
   s.username,
   sum(h.wait_time + h.time_waited ) "total wait time"
from
   v$active_session_history     h,
   v$session                    s,
   v$event_name                 e
where
   h.session_id = s.sid
and
   e.event_id = h.event_id
and
   e.wait_class <> 'Idle'
and
   s.username IS NOT NULL
group by
   s.sid, s.username
order by
   3;
```

This sample output shows the total wait time, both by process ID (SID) and by individual users.

```
     SID    USERNAME             total wait time
  ---------- ---------------     ---------------
     261    SYS                        1,537,288
     259    SYS                       12,247,007
     254    SYS                       18,640,736
```

Here is the script that is commonly used for exception reporting of wait events.

Using Active Session History (ASH) for Troubleshooting   **165**

🖫 * ash_event_rollup.sql

```
ttitle 'High waits on events|Rollup by hour'


column mydate heading 'Yr. Mo Dy Hr' format a13;
column event format a30;
column total_waits heading 'tot waits' format 999,999;
column time_waited heading 'time wait' format 999,999;
column total_timeouts heading 'timeouts' format 9,999;
break on to_char(snap_time,'yyyy-mm-dd') skip 1;

select
to_char(e.sample_time,'yyyy-mm-dd HH24') mydate,
e.event,
count(e.event) total_waits,
sum(e.time_waited) time_waited
from
v$active_session_history e
where
e.event not like '%timer'
and
e.event not like '%message%'
and
e.event not like '%slave wait%'
having
count(e.event) > 100
group by
to_char(e.sample_time,'yyyy-mm-dd HH24'),
e.event
order by 1
;
```

The output from this script is shown next. A time-series report is the result, showing those days and hours when the thresholds are exceeded. Notice that every evening between 10:00 PM and 11:00 PM, high I/O waits on the Oracle redo logs are being experienced.

```
Wed Aug 21 page 1
High waits on events
Rollup by hour

Yr. Mo Dy Hr    EVENT                       tot waits    time wait
------------    --------------------------  ---------    ---------
2002-08-18 22   LGWR wait for redo copy         9,326        1,109
2002-08-18 23   LGWR wait for redo copy         8,506          316
2002-08-18 23   buffer busy waits                 214       21,388
2002-08-19 00   LGWR wait for redo copy           498            5
2002-08-19 01   LGWR wait for redo copy           497           15
2002-08-19 22   LGWR wait for redo copy         9,207        1,433
2002-08-19 22   buffer busy waits                 529       53,412
2002-08-19 23   LGWR wait for redo copy         9,066          367
2002-08-19 23   buffer busy waits                 250       24,479
2002-08-20 00   LGWR wait for redo copy           771           16
```

```
2002-08-20 22   LGWR wait for redo copy        8,030      2,013
2002-08-20 22   buffer busy waits                356     35,583
2002-08-20 23   LGWR wait for redo copy        8,021        579
2002-08-20 23   buffer busy waits                441     44,677
2002-08-21 00   LGWR wait for redo copy        1,013         26
2002-08-21 00   rdbms ipc reply                  160     30,986
2002-08-21 01   LGWR wait for redo copy          541         17
```

The next sample query against the AWR ASH table shows a list of database objects that caused the most wait times during time interval stored in AWR. Idle wait times are not included in the output.

🖫   **< ash_object_wait_time.sql**

```
select
   o.owner,
   o.object_name,
   o.object_type,
   SUM(h.wait_time + h.time_waited ) "total wait time"
from
   v$active_session_history        h,
   dba_objects                     o,
   v$event_name                    e
where
   h.current_obj# = o.object_id
and
   e.event_id = h.event_id
and
   e.wait_class <> 'Idle'
group by
   o.owner,
   o.object_name,
   o.object_type
order by
   4 DESC;
```

This report produces a list of hot objects which might be candidates for further tuning investigations:

```
                       Object              Object
OWNER                  Name                Type        total wait time
---------------------  ------------------  ----------  ---------------
SYSMAN                 MGMT_OMS_PARAMETERS  TABLE           1,1232E+10
SYS                    SCHEDULER$_WINDOW_DE TABLE              2989867
                       TAILS

SYSMAN                 MPVV_PK              INDEX              1333198
SYSMAN                 MGMT_DELTA_ENTRY_SHO INDEX               835641
                       ULD_BE_UK

SYSMAN                 MGMT_DB_LATEST_HDM_F TABLE               397504
                       INDINGS
```

SYS	CDEF$	TABLE	116853
SYS	I_LINK1	INDEX	46922
SYS	SYS_IOT_TOP_8542	INDEX	25469
SYS	I_COM1	INDEX	24908
SYS	I_CDEF3	INDEX	23125
SYSMAN	MGMT_DB_LATEST_HDM_F INDINGS	INDEX	11325
SYS	I_OBJ2	INDEX	5953
SYS	WRH$_ACTIVE_SESSION_ HISTORY_BL	TABLE	304
SYSTEM	SQLPLUS_PRODUCT_PROF ILE	TABLE	3

With *v$active_session_history*, there is now the ability to trace sessions without using the 10046 event to extended trace.

How can the information available through the *v$active_session_history* view be used? If a session that is experiencing delays or hangs has been identified and the goal is to identify the SQL statement(s) the session is issuing, along with the wait events being experienced for a particular time period, a query similar to this one can be issued:

```
Select  C.sql text,
        B.name,
        count(*),
        sum(time_waited)
from    v$active_session_history A,
        v$event_name B,
        v$sqlarea C
where   A.sample_time between '10-JUL-04 09:57:00 PM' and
                             '10-JUL-04 09:59:00 PM' and
        A.event# = b.event#
and
        A.session_id= 123
and
        A.sql_id = C.sql_id
group by
        C.sql_text, B.name
```

The *current_obj#* column can be joined with the *dba_objects* view to get name of the object, or it can be joined with the *current_file#* column using *dba_data_files* to see the name of datafile that was accessed. Even a particular block that caused a wait event can be identified using the *current_block#* column.

It is also possible to identify hot datafiles, objects, or even data blocks that are being accessed by sessions more frequently than others and thus could be candidates for additional investigations. The *hot_files_ash.sql* query shows hot datafiles that caused the most wait times during session access:

hot_files_ash.sql

```
select
  f.file_name        "Data File",
  count(*)           "Wait Number",
  sum(h.time_waited) "Total Time Waited"
from
  v$active_session_history h,
  dba_data_files          f
where
  h.current_file# = f.file_id
group by
  f.file_name
order by
  3 DESC
```

The sample output looks like:

Data File	Wait Number	Total Time Waited
D:\ORACLE\ORADATA\DBDABR\SYSAUX01.DBF	5514	994398837
D:\ORACLE\ORADATA\DBDABR\SYSTEM01.DBF	2579	930483678
D:\ORACLE\ORADATA\DBDABR\UNDOTBS01.DBF	245	7727218
D:\ORACLE\ORADATA\DBDABR\USERS01.DBF	141	1548274

Note that the *v$active_session_history* view does not catch session activity that is extremely fast, but it should catch activity that causes the most waits and resource consumption.

Below are several helpful queries that run against the *v$active_session_history* view. The first query, *events_waits_hr_ask.sql*, shows resources that were in high demand in the last hour.

events_waits_hr_ash.sql

```
select
  h.event "Wait Event",
  sum(h.wait_time + h.time_waited) "Total Wait Time"
from
  v$active_session_history h,
  v$event_name e
where
```

```
      h.sample_time BETWEEN sysdate - 1/24 AND sysdate
and
  h.event_id = e.event_id
and
  e.wait_class <> 'Idle'
group by
  h.event
order by
  2 desc
```

The output looks like the following:

```
Wait Event                           Total Wait Time
------------------------------------ ---------------
Queue Monitor Task Wait                   10,256,950
class slave wait                          10,242,904
log file switch completion                 5,142,555
control file parallel write                4,813,121
db file sequential read                      334,871
process startup                              232,137
log file sync                                203,087
latch free                                    36,934
log buffer space                              25,090
latch: redo allocation                        22,444
db file parallel write                           714
db file scattered read                           470
log file parallel write                          182
direct path read temp                            169
control file sequential read                     160
direct path write temp                           112
```

Display SQL Wait Details in ASH

Now see how ASH data can be transformed to give a complete picture of system wait details. The following ASH script can be used to find details about the most active SQL in the past 10 minutes:

🖫 **ash_sql_counts.sql**

```
col c1 heading "invocation|count"    format 9,999
col c2 heading "percentage|of|load"  format 99

select
  sql_id, count(*)                          c1,
  round(count(*)/sum(count(*)) over (), 2)  c2
from
  v$active_session_history
where
  sample_time > sysdate - 1/24/60
and
  session_type <> 'BACKGROUND'
group by
  sql_id
```

```
order by
   count(*) desc;
```

```
SQL_ID            COUNTS    PCTLOAD
-------------     --------  --------
25wtt4ycbtkyz         456     32.95
7umwqvcy7tusf         123      8.89
01vunx6d35khz         119      8.6
bdyq2uph07cmp         102      7.37
```

In this example, the script's output shows that the *sql_id* of 25wtt4ycbtkyz was the most active SQL during the past 10 minutes, executed 456 times. This *sql_id* can be used to join into other ASH views to see more details about that specific SQL statement.

To show SQL with the most I/O, join *v$active_session_history* into *v$event_name* to display the SQL ID for all SQL statements that are waiting on user I/O.

🖫 ash_sql_waiting_io.sql

```
select
   ash.sql_id,
   count(*)
from
   v$active_session_history ash,
   v$event_name            evt
where
   ash.sample_time > sysdate - 1/24/60
and
   ash.session_state = 'WAITING'
and
   ash.event_id = evt.event_id
and
   evt.wait_class = 'User I/O'
group by
   sql_id
order by
   count(*) desc;
```

```
SQL_ID            COUNT(*)
-------------     --------
5a8s3s46u2ra7            1
```

This ASH report is useful for finding the root causes of sudden spikes or transient performance problems, but the query must be run quickly, within five minutes of the slowdown. Note that this ASH report has information that includes current transaction IDs (the key) plus blocking session details, top sessions, SQL details and wait event details.

Even though these ASH queries look quite simple, do not underestimate their complexity and value as a reactive tuning aid. There are many complexities buried in ASH. Although ASH provides innovative ways to collect and use real-time performance information, it is not perfect, and there are special cases where ASH might not yield the expected information. For example, the times in the *dba_hist_active_sess_history* are the sampled times, and as such, they are not statistically valid for the SQL avg, min, or max operators.

Tip - wait_time vs. time_waited

Do not be fooled by similar-sounding ASH metrics! For example, consider the differences between *wait_time* and *time_waited* in *v$active_session_history*:

- *wait_time*: The *wait_time* metric is the same as the *wait_time* found in *v$session_wait*. A value of zero (0) indicates "waiting", while any other non-zero value means "on cpu".

- *time_waited*: The *time_ waited* metric is the actual time waited for any in-flight event, and it is updated when the event is completed.

With this basic picture of ASH, the next step is to move deeper and see how to conduct a wait event analysis with ASH data.

Event Wait Analysis with ASH

With ASH tables, a snapshot of Oracle wait events can be collected every hour and plot changes all of the changes in wait behavior over time, seeking visual trends. It is also possible to set thresholds and report only on wait events that exceed the predefined threshold. For example, the following script can be commonly used for exception reporting of wait events.

🖫 ash_high_wait_events.sql

```
ttitle 'High waits on events|Rollup by hour'


column mydate heading 'Yr.  Mo Dy Hr'     format a13;
column event                              format a30;
column total_waits     heading 'tot waits' format 999,999;
column time_waited     heading 'time wait' format 999,999;
column total_timeouts heading 'timeouts'  format 9,999;

break on to_char(snap_time,'yyyy-mm-dd') skip 1;
 select
   to_char(e.sample_time,'yyyy-mm-dd HH24')   mydate,
   e.event,
   count(e.event)                             total_waits,
   sum(e.time_waited)                         time_waited
from
   v$active_session_history e
where
   e.event not like '%timer'
and
   e.event not like '%message%'
and
   e.event not like '%slave wait%'
having
   count(e.event) > 100
group by
   to_char(e.sample_time,'yyyy-mm-dd HH24'),
   e.event
order by 1
;
```

The output below is from this script. The result is a time-series, showing those days and hours when set thresholds are exceeded. From this listing, it is easy to see that every evening between 10:00 PM and 11:00 PM, the system experiences high waits on the redo logs.

```
Wed Aug 21                                        page   1
                     High waits on events
                        Rollup by hour

Yr.  Mo Dy Hr EVENT                        tot waits time wait
------------ ------------------------------ --------- ---------
2002-08-18 22 LGWR wait for redo copy         9,326     1,109
2002-08-18 23 LGWR wait for redo copy         8,506       316
2002-08-18 23 buffer busy waits                214    21,388
2002-08-19 00 LGWR wait for redo copy          498         5
2002-08-19 01 LGWR wait for redo copy          497        15
2002-08-19 22 LGWR wait for redo copy         9,207     1,433
```

```
2002-08-19 22 buffer busy waits                    529   53,412
2002-08-19 23 LGWR wait for redo copy            9,066      367
2002-08-19 23 buffer busy waits                    250   24,479
2002-08-20 00 LGWR wait for redo copy              771       16
2002-08-20 22 LGWR wait for redo copy            8,030    2,013
2002-08-20 22 buffer busy waits                    356   35,583
2002-08-20 23 LGWR wait for redo copy            8,021      579
2002-08-20 23 buffer busy waits                    441   44,677
2002-08-21 00 LGWR wait for redo copy            1,013       26
2002-08-21 00 rdbms ipc reply                      160   30,986
2002-08-21 01 LGWR wait for redo copy              541       17
```

The Oracle Wait Event Interface within Ion gives the ability to monitor database bottlenecks in real time and OEM becomes even more powerful when used together with the AWR tables (Figure 8.3).

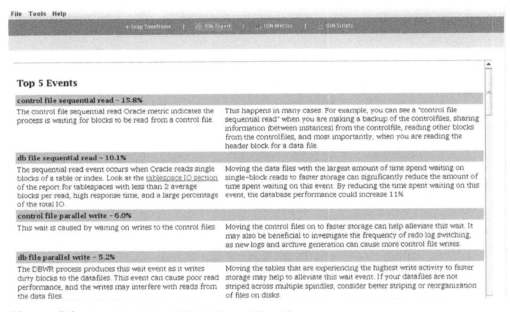

Figure 8.3: *Ion Display of Wait Event Details*

Now it is time to explore the subtleties of the ASH tables. Prior to Oracle 10g, there was no standard way to keep and analyze the history for a session's wait events into the Oracle database kernel. Instead, DBAs had to write custom code to vacuum wait information from the *v$* views and store them inside STATSPACK extension tables.

This inability to capture information was critical to evaluating database performance because most wait events that occurred in real time were not caught using manual queries. This lack of a quick interface caused Oracle DBAs to develop custom tools to monitor their wait events in an automated manner.

The Performance Overhead of Collecting ASH Data

Remember, the ASH data collection mechanism keeps highly detailed session information for a short period of time. ASH data is filtered out by writing it to permanent AWR tables using the MMON background process every 30 minutes. However, also recognize that ASH is part of the extra-cost performance pack and diagnostic packs, costing $6,000 per CPU, as of 2009. While Oracle ASH relieves the DBA from the problem of collecting their own dynamic performance information, there are alternatives, and many shops choose to collect their own data directly from the SGA, the $x\$$ structures and from the $v\$$ views. Now see how the collection mechanism can be built and money can be saved on licensing fees.

Within the world of molecular physics, the scientists say that the act of observing a subatomic behavior will alter the behavior, and there is the same problem with Oracle system monitoring. In the nanosecond world of the Oracle SGA, the act of running SQL to collect statistics from the $v\$$ views can easily exceed the cost of the instruction itself.

Before investing in real-time monitors to replace or supplement ASH, be aware of several potential problems:

- On stressed systems, greedy real-time monitors can create more performance problems than they reveal.

- There are few options to remedy an acute performance problem. It can be difficult, if not impossible, to correct some acute performance problems.

Using ASH to Trace a Session

The *v$active_session_history* view can fully replace the 10046 trace event. So look at the *v$active_session_history* columns *wait_time*, *session_state* and *time_waited*.

If *wait_time* is zero, the session currently has a *session_state* of WAITING, and the event listed is the event that is the last event waited for before this sample. The *time_waited* is the amount of time that the session waited for the event listed in the event field.

If *wait_time* is greater than zero, the session currently has a *session_state* of ON CPU, and the event listed is the event that was last waited for before this sample. The *time_waited* will be zero. *Time_waited* will only contain a value when waits are occurring at the instant the sample is taken. For clarity, this means that if *wait_time* in one row is two, the *session_state* will be ON CPU and the *time_waited* will be zero. The value of two in *wait_time* represents the time spent waiting the last time it waited before the current time on the CPU.

In order to use ASH, the DBA will need to understand the layout of the views. Figure 8.4 shows the connection between the *v$session* data, the key ASH view named *v$active_session_history*, and the AWR structure named *wrh$_active_session_history*. The underlined fields can be used to join the other views to gather the specific information needed to diagnose performance problems.

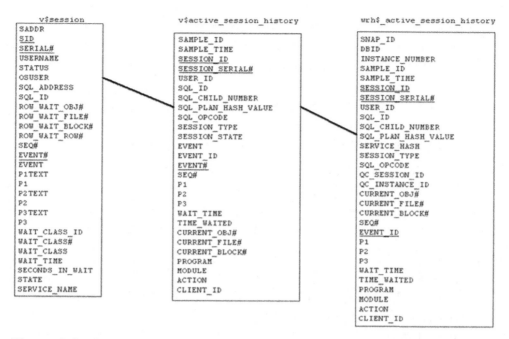

Figure 8.4: *Relationships Among v$session and Other Structures*

Due to the volume of data that can be found in *v$active_session_history* during times of heavy activity, not all of the data is stored in the AWR tables. This is because of the dirty read mechanism which reads data even though it may belong to an in-process transaction. This allows the impact on the database to be negligible. In spite of this limitation, enough data is kept to allow the ASH information to be statistically accurate and useful for historical review.

For example, using the query below, SQL statements that accessed the orders table for session number 74 on the current day can be identified:

```
select
   h.sql_id,
   s.sql_text
from
   dba_hist_active_sess_history h,
   v$sql                        s
where
   h.session_id = 74
AND
```

```
    h.sql_id = s.sql_id
AND
    TRUNC(h.sample_time) = TRUNC(SYSDATE)
AND
    s.sql_fulltext like '%orders%';
```

The output of this query shows the actual SQL statements executed against the orders table. This output is truncated to only one record that was retrieved due to the large amount of data available:

```
SQL_ID      SQL_TEXT
----------- ----------------------------------------------------------------------------------
4g5qdabvfumhc select c.c_day wrk_date, c.day_type, nvl(c.rl_day, 'N') rl_day, nvl(c.short_day,
            'N') short_day, c.week_day,        p.id ewp_id, p.emp_id, p.dep_id, p.flag_main,
            p.eca_id, p.emp_sal, p.sal_prc,       nvl(d.start_date, p.start_date) start_date,
            nvl(nvl(d.finish_date, p.finish_date), to_date('9999', 'yyyy')) finish_date,
            d.id wpd_id, d.wsc_id, d.team_num, d.ept_id,        (select decode(c.day_type, 'W',
```

The output above shows the SQL that was issued against the orders table. Since this application produces the same set of SQL statements against the database, the DBA can go further and determine what SQL statements issued against the orders table were issued most frequently in the recent past.

These SQL statements are the most likely candidates for further investigations in order to find an effective way to reduce buffer busy waits events. The following is the query that retrieves the most frequent SQL statements identifiers against the orders table:

Do not cause a performance problem!

Repeated querying of the *v$sql* view causes memory access against the library latch once for each retrieved row. Be careful!

🖫 ash_count_table_usage.sql

```
select
    h.sql_id,
    count(*)
from
    dba_hist_active_sess_history h,
    v$sql                        s
where
```

```
   h.sql_id = s.sql_id
and
   s.sql_fulltext like '%orders%'
having
   count(*) > 1
group by
   h.sql_id
order by
   2 DESC;
```

The output of the above query yields the following results:

```
SQL_ID          COUNT(*)
-------------   ----------
3ta4tz9xbn4gf      2,678
fxr47mpnpc2yx        740
```

The actual SQL statements can now be retrieved from the *v$sql* view
using the SQL identifiers obtained above and then a deeper investigation
can be conducted of those suspect SQL statements. The example above
gives an idea of one possible usage of the ASH feature in a real tuning
session.

Now take a look at the *v$* views that accumulate task-level data and see
how ASH is built up from this data.

Inside the *v$session_wait_history*

Now that *v$active_session_history* has been covered, compare it to the
v$session_wait_history view.   As can be guessed from the name,
v$session_wait_history is a history table and it contains the last ten wait
events for every current database session. Here are the columns:

```
SQL> desc v$session_wait_history

Name                    Null?     Type
--------------------    --------  -----------
SID                               NUMBER
SEQ#                              NUMBER
EVENT#                            NUMBER
EVENT                             VARCHAR2(64)
P1TEXT                           VARCHAR2(64)
P1                                NUMBER
P2TEXT                           VARCHAR2(64)
P2                                NUMBER
P3TEXT                           VARCHAR2(64)
```

P3	NUMBER
WAIT_TIME	NUMBER
WAIT_COUNT	NUMBER

If any session in *v$session_wait_history* is focused on using the SID, it shows the wait event details for that session.

In this example, assume that session 74 had high buffer busy waits. Drill into *v$session_wait_history* where *v$session_wait_history.sid*=74. Also, note the join into *v$session* to get the username and the extraction of some special columns, namely P1 and P2:

💾 **session_wait_history_events.sql**

```
select
   swh.seq#        seq_nbr,
   sess.sid        sid,
   sess.username   username,
   swh.event       event,
   swh.p1,
   swh.p2
from
   v$session                 sess,
   v$session_wait_history    swh
where
   sess.sid = 74
and
   sess.sid = swh.sid
order by
   swh.seq#;
```

Now see some additional latch events:

SEQ#	SID	USERNAME	EVENT	P1	P2
1	74	PCS	buffer busy waits	3	21277
2	74	PCS	latch: cache buffers chains	1556332118	172
3	74	PCS	latch: cache buffers chains	1556332118	172
4	74	PCS	buffer busy waits	4	155

By querying the *v$session_wait_history* view, it becomes clear that session 74 experienced some additional waits. But where? How can it be known what table or index block is experiencing this contention?

In this example, P1 and P2 were resolved for the *object_name* and *object_type* for the block, and it is apparent that these were buffer busy waits for an UNDO segment. Also, it appears that the session had many waits for cache buffer chain latch. This type of contention has two likely causes: very long buffer chains or very heavy access to the same data blocks. Usually, this flavor of buffer contention is caused by identical SQL queries being issued by numerous sessions, all of which retrieve rows from the same set of data blocks.

The tuning options available in this situation are to either tune the SQL statement or application so that it will access the data blocks less often, i.e. cache the data inside the application. Another approach is to spread the data across many data blocks by setting *pctused* to a high value such as 90, thereby allowing only a few rows in each data block before the block is taken off the freelist. This spreads the hot rows across more data blocks.

The next step in reactive troubleshooting is to determine what SQL statements the session executed the fetches from the orders table. Finally, the exact bullock number is found within the table.
This is where the friendly *v$active_session_history* comes to the rescue. Unlike the *v$session_wait_history*, the extra-cost *v$active_session_history* table has much finer sampling, and snapshots of a sessions' activities can be seen every second. Nevertheless, ASH does not have to be used. Take a look at the free view, *v$event_name*.

To understand the state changes during task execution, one should distinguish between active and idle states. A database session is active when it waits for any non-idle event or when it is waiting on CPU. Idle events are indicated by the *wait_class* column for the corresponding wait event in the *v$event_name* view. This view reports one row per active session for every snapshot taken. Table 8.1 shows the contents of *v$event_name*:

snap_id	UNIQUE SNAPSHOT ID
dbid	Database ID for the snapshot
instance_number	Instance number for the snapshot
sample_id	ID of the sample
sample_time	Time of the sample
session_id	Session identifier

snap_id	UNIQUE SNAPSHOT ID
session_serial#	Session serial number
user_id	Oracle user identifier
sql_id	SQL identifier of the SQL statement *sql_child_number*. Child number of the SQL statement
sql_opcode	Indicates what phase of operation the SQL statement is in
current_obj#	Object ID of the object that the session is currently referencing
current_file#	File number of the file containing the block that the session is currently referencing
current_block#	ID of the block that the session is currently referencing
event_id	Identifier of the resource or event for which the session is waiting or for which the session last waited
wait_time	Total wait time for the event for which the session last waited
time_waited	Time that the current session actually spent waiting for the event.
program	Name of the operating system program
module	Name of the currently executing module
client_id	Client identifier of the session
snap_id	Unique snapshot ID

Table 8.1: *Contents of the v$event_name View*

The information available in this view allows the determination of which SQL statement was executed at a given time, what wait event the sessions waited for, and what database file, object, or data block was accessed.

Now that how to extract wait events has been shown, the next step will be how they can be used for signature analysis.

Signature Analysis of ASH Wait Events

There are many more benefits that can be achieved using information provided by the ASH as it is a useful tool for database activity analysis and performance tuning. The two sample analytical reports following make use of the ASH *v$active_session_history* view.

Signature analysis is an important area of Oracle tuning and one that especially applies to time-series wait event analysis. Just as Socrates said

"Know Thy Self", the Oracle DBA must "Know Thy Database". Signature analysis is ideal for wait event tuning, particularly in the areas of:

- Spotting hidden trends

- Allowing holistic tuning

- Allowing just-in-time anticipation and self-tuning using the *dbms_scheduler* package

- Allowing adjustment of object characteristics such as freelists, file placement, caching, and block population

The following script compares the wait event values from *dba_hist_waitstat* and *dba_hist_active_sess_history*. This allows the identification of the exact objects that are experiencing wait events.

💾 ash_display_table_index_wait_counts.sql

```
set pages 999
set lines 80

break on snap_time skip 2

col snap_time      heading 'Snap|Time'     format a20
col file_name      heading 'File|Name'     format a40
col object_type    heading 'Object|Type'   format a10
col object_name    heading 'Object|Name'   format a20
col wait_count     heading 'Wait|Count'    format 999,999
col time           heading 'Time'          format 999,999

select
   to_char(begin_interval_time,'yyyy-mm-dd hh24:mi') snap_time,
--   file_name,
   object_type,
   object_name,
   wait_count,
   time
from
   dba_hist_waitstat              wait,
   dba_hist_snapshot              snap,
   dba_hist_active_sess_history   ash,
   dba_data_files                 df,
   dba_objects                    obj
where
   wait.snap_id = snap.snap_id
and
   wait.snap_id = ash.snap_id
and
   df.file_id = ash.current_file#
and
```

```
   obj.object_id = ash.current_obj#
and
   wait_count > 50
order by
   to_char(begin_interval_time,'yyyy-mm-dd hh24:mi'),
   file_name
;
```

This script is enabled to join into the *dba_data_files* view to get the file names associated with the wait event. This is a very powerful script that can be used to quickly drill in to find the cause of specific waits. Below is a sample output:

```
SQL> @ash_display_table_index_wait_counts.sql
```

This will compare values from *dba_hist_waitstat* with detailed information from *dba_hist_active_sess_history*.

Snap Time	Object Type	Object Name	Wait Count	Time
2004-02-28 01:00	TABLE	ORDOR	4,273	67
	INDEX	PK_CUST_ID	12,373	324
	INDEX	FK_CUST_NAME	3,883	17
	INDEX	PK_ITEM_ID	1,256	967
2004-02-29 03:00	TABLE	ITEM_DETAIL	83	69
2004-03-01 04:00	TABLE	ITEM_DETAIL	1,246	45
2004-03-01 21:00	TABLE	CUSTOMER_DET	4,381	354
	TABLE	IND_PART	117	15
2004-03-04 01:00	TABLE	MARVIN	41,273	16
	TABLE	FACTOTUM	2,827	43
	TABLE	DOW_KNOB	853	6
	TABLE	ITEM_DETAIL	57	331
	TABLE	HIST_ORD	4,337	176
	TABLE	TAB_HIST	127	66

The first analytic trend report yields total wait times by the hour of a day. The following script shows when database sessions have to wait for resources that decrease response time:

🖫 ash_cpu_foregound_events.sql

```
select
   TO_CHAR(h.sample_time,'HH24') "Hour",
   Sum(h.wait_time/100)          "Total Wait Time (Sec)"
from
   v$active_session_history     h,
   v$event_name                 n
where
   h.session_state = 'ON CPU'
and
   h.session_type = 'FOREGROUND'
and
   h.event_id = n.EVENT_ID
and
   n.wait_class <> 'Idle'
group by
   TO_CHAR(h.sample_time,'HH24');
```

The output of this query might look like the results listed below, and it shows a distinct signature or repeating wait event pattern within the database. This signature will be valid for the entire range of ASH snapshots that is chosen to retain. Many DBAs will retain several months' worth of ASH data so they can perform system-wide wait event tuning.

```
SQL> @ash_cpu_foregound_events.sql


Hr Total Wait Time (Sec)
-- --------------------
1                    219
2                302,998
3                 60,982
4                169,716
5                 39,593
6                299,953
7                122,933
8                  5,147
```

From the above listing, it appears that the database had the most wait times at 12AM and 4PM.

Most Oracle databases also have daily signatures with regularly repeating trends in wait events. In the same manner, the following query that reports total wait times by the day of the week could be run:

🖫 ash_cpu_foregound_events_dow.sql

```
select
   TO_CHAR(h.sample_time,'Day')  "Hour",
   sum(h.wait_time/100)          "Total Wait Time (Sec)"
from
   v$active_session_history      h,
   v$event_name                  n
where
   h.session_state = 'ON CPU'
and
   h.session_type = 'FOREGROUND'
and
   h.event_id = n.EVENT_ID
and
   n.wait_class <> 'Idle'
group by
   TO_CHAR(h.sample_time,'Day');
```

This query produces a listing that looks like the one shown next:

```
Hour        Total Wait Time (Sec)
---------   ---------------------
Monday                    679,089
Tuesday                   141,142
Wednesday                 181,226
Thursday                  241,711
Friday                    319,023
Saturday                   93,362
Sunday                     81,086
```

From this output, it is clear that the database is most stressed on Monday, and the numbers can be visualized by pasting them into a spreadsheet and plotting them with the chart wizard. The results from the two trend reports just given allow the DBA to further investigate ASH data in order to get more detailed information. The query below retrieves a list of wait events that had high wait time from 12AM to 1PM.

A previous report on the same system showed that sessions experienced high wait times during this time period.

```
select
   h.event              "Wait Event",
   SUM(h.wait_time/100) "Wait Time (Sec)"
from
   v$active_session_history      h,
   v$event_name                  n
where
   h.session_state = 'ON CPU'
```

```
and
   h.session_type = 'FOREGROUND'
and
   h.event_id = n.EVENT_ID
and
   to_char(h.sample_time,'HH24') = '12'
and
   n.wait_class <> 'Idle'
group by
   h.event
order by
 2 DESC;
```

This query returns results that look like the following, showing aggregate totals for important wait events.

```
Wait Event                     Wait Time (Sec)
-----------------------------  ---------------
buffer busy waits                      522,152
db file sequential read                299,572
SQL*Net more data to client                317
SQL*Net more data from client              201
SQL*Net message to client                   55
```

From the listing above, it can be concluded that between 12AM and 1PM the database sessions waited most for *buffer busy waits* and *db file sequential read* events, indicating table access by index.

After these results are acquired, the DBA can determine what SQL statements were issued during this time period and probably find ones that may cause buffer cache contention or heavy disk read access. The ASH provides the Oracle DBA with the ability to build different trend reports in order to observe database activity from various points of view.

The AWR repository stores snapshots for the ASH view called *v$active_session_history* in its internal table *wrh$_active_session_history*. This table is available to DBAs through the *dba_hist_active_sess_history* view. The AWR does not store snapshots of ASH activity on a continuous basis. This means that the *wrh$_active_session_history* table stores sessions' activity records that were in the SGA circular buffer at the time the AWR snapshot was taken.

This data archiving approach does not allow monitoring activity for particular sessions because the AWR misses all the activity that occurred in the session during the period of time between two AWR snapshots. However, trend reports based on data exposed by *dba_hist_active_sess_history* view can be built. The following pages will present information on valuable trend analysis that can be performed against the AWR concerning ASH activity.

It is possible to identify hot datafiles or database objects that were accessed by sessions more frequently than others. These hot datafiles or database objects could be candidates for additional tuning investigations. The following query shows hot datafiles that caused the most wait times during access:

```
select
    f.file_name          "Data File",
    COUNT(*)             "Wait Number",
    SUM(h.time_waited)   "Total Time Waited"
from
    v$active_session_history     h,
    dba_data_files               f
where
    h.current_file# = f.file_id
group by
    f.file_name
order by 3 DESC;
```

This query produces output like the following:

Data File	Wait Number	Total Time Waited
D:\ORACLE\ORADATA\DBDABR\SYSAUX01.DBF	153	11,169,771
D:\ORACLE\ORADATA\DBDABR\SYSTEM01.DBF	222	6,997,212
D:\ORACLE\ORADATA\DBDABR\UNDOTBS01.DBF	45	1,758,065

The datafile named *d:\oracle\oradata\dbdabr\sysaux01.dbf* had the highest wait time during access to its data. This might indicate the need to further investigate SQL statements that are accessing data within this datafile or the need to spread its content between several datafiles, thus eliminating a possible hot spot.

The Oracle multiple data buffers or the KEEP pool could also be used to reduce waits on these objects by caching them in the data buffers. If there are high waits on in-buffer reads, the SQL that accesses the hot object needs to be tuned to reduce the amount of logical I/O.

The next query against the *dba_hist_active_sess_history* view reports a list of resources that were in high demand in the last hour. This query does not reflect idle wait events.

```
select
   e.name                          "Wait Event",
   SUM(h.wait_time + h.time_waited) "Total Wait Time"
from
   v$active_session_history        h,
   v$event_name                    e
where
   h.event_id = e.event_id
and
   e.wait_class <> 'Idle'
group by
   e.name
order by 2 DESC;
```

This query produces a listing like the one below, showing aggregate wait time for each event:

```
Wait Event                        Total Wait Time
-----------------------------     ---------------
log buffer space                        9,638,484
db file sequential read                 8,442,918
log file switch completion              5,231,711
write complete waits                    5,200,368
db file scattered read                  4452,153
process startup                         3623,464
rdbms ipc reply                           917,765
log file sync                             662,224
latch free                                550,241
latch: library cache                      370,696
db file parallel write                    364,641
free buffer waits                         319,151
latch: redo allocation                     64,984
LGWR wait for redo copy                    63,647
read by other session                      52,757
log file sequential read                   46,126
null event                                 33,011
log file parallel write                    26,280
SQL*Net more data to client                 8,894
latch: cache buffers chains                 7,005
control file sequential read                3,966
direct path read temp                         395
direct path write temp                        229
SQL*Net message to client                      74
```

From the listing above, it can be seen that there is an issue with the log buffer space wait event that may indicate the need to increase the *log_buffer* parameter to increase the cache in order to minimize this possible bottleneck.

Using the AWR ASH view, the DBA can also retrieve a list of database users who have experienced high wait times during the time period between any two snapshots. The following query can be used to identify these target users:

```
select
   s.sid,
   s.username,
   sum(h.wait_time + h.time_waited) "total wait time"
from
   v$active_session_history      h,
   v$session                     s,
   v$event_name                  e
where
   h.session_id = s.sid
and
   e.event_id = h.event_id
and
   e.wait_class <> 'Idle'
and
   s.username IS NOT NULL
group by
   s.sid, s.username
order by 3;
```

This sample output shows the total wait time, both by process ID (SID) and by individual users.

```
      SID   USERNAME           total wait time
-----------  ---------------   ---------------
      261   SYS                      1,537,288
      259   SYS                     12,247,007
      254   SYS                     18,640,736
```

The next sample query against the AWR ASH table shows a list of database objects that caused the most wait times during time interval stored in AWR. Idle wait times are not included in the output.

```
select
   o.owner,
   o.object_name,
   o.object_type,
```

```
      SUM(h.wait_time + h.time_waited) "total wait time"
from
    v$active_session_history      h,
    dba_objects                   o,
    v$event_name                  e
where
    h.current_obj# = o.object_id
and
    e.event_id = h.event_id
and
    e.wait_class <> 'Idle'
group by
    o.owner,
    o.object_name,
    o.object_type
order by
    4 DESC;
```

This report produces a list of hot objects which might be candidates for further tuning investigations:

OWNER	Object Name	Object Type	total wait time
SYSMAN	MGMT_OMS_PARAMETERS	TABLE	1,1232E+10
SYS	SCHEDULER$_WINDOW_DE TAILS	TABLE	2989867
SYSMAN	MPVV_PK	INDEX	1333198
SYSMAN	MGMT_DELTA_ENTRY_SHO ULD_BE_UK	INDEX	835641
SYSMAN	MGMT_DB_LATEST_HDM_F INDINGS	TABLE	397504
SYS	CDEF$	TABLE	116853
SYS	I_LINK1	INDEX	46922
SYS	SYS_IOT_TOP_8542	INDEX	25469
SYS	I_COM1	INDEX	24908
SYS	I_CDEF3	INDEX	23125
SYSMAN	MGMT_DB_LATEST_HDM_F INDINGS	INDEX	11325
SYS	I_OBJ2	INDEX	5953
SYS	WRH$_ACTIVE_SESSION_ HISTORY_BL	TABLE	304
SYSTEM	SQLPLUS_PRODUCT_PROF ILE	TABLE	3

As part of Oracle's commitment to time-series tuning, 10g contains major changes in the *x$* structures as well as many new and modified *v$*

performance views. Figure 8.5 shows the 10g *v$* views relating to database events.

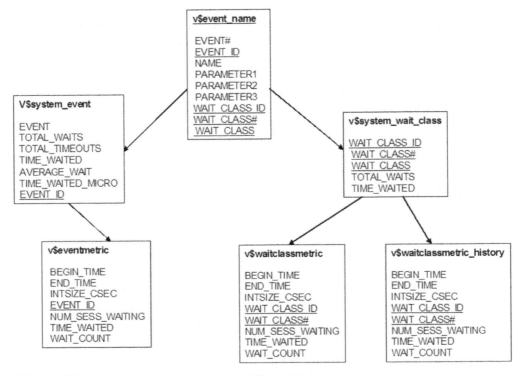

Figure 8.5: *The Oracle 10g v$ System Event Structure*

Now explore how the ASH information can be viewed from inside Oracle Enterprise Manager (OEM).

Using ASH in OEM

Together, the AWR and ASH metrics form the foundation for a complete Oracle tuning framework, and the Enterprise Manager provides a great tool for visualizing the bottlenecks. Now that the underlying wait event collection mechanism has been explained, it is time to explore how OEM gives an intelligent window into this critical Oracle tuning information.

Before the use of OEM to identify a performance issue is examined, it must be noted that the AWR and ASH information can be used inside OEM to create customized exception alerts. Even when the DBA is not watching, OEM can send an e-mail warning about any impending performance issue. Figure 8.6 shows the ASH alert threshold screen:

▼ Wait Bottlenecks	None
Active Sessions	Not Set
Active Sessions Using CPU	Not Set
Active Sessions Using CPU (%)	Not Set
Active Sessions Waiting: I/O	Not Set
Active Sessions Waiting: I/O (%)	Not Set
Active Sessions Waiting: Other	Not Set
Active Sessions Waiting: Other (%)	Not Set
Average Instance CPU (%)	Not Set
CPU Time (sec)	Not Set
Wait Time (%)	Not Set
Wait Time (sec)	Not Set

Figure 8.6: *OEM ASH Wait Bottleneck Metrics*

This is an especially important screen for customizing OEM alerts because thresholds can be set based on changes with either absolute of delta-based metrics. For example, it may be desirable to have OEM alert the DBA when the following session metrics are exceeded:

- Active sessions waiting: I/O: Alert when there are more than 500 active sessions waiting on I/O

- Active sessions waiting: I/O (%): Alert when active sessions waiting on I/O increases by more than 10%

- Wait time (sec): Alert when wait time exceeds two seconds

- Wait time (%): Alert when wait time increases by more than 25%

The new OEM also allows the viewing of session wait information at the metric level. For example, if OEM informs the user that the major wait event in the database is related to concurrency such as locks, latches, and pins, the DBA can drill down on the concurrency link to go to the OEM active sessions waiting screen as shown in Figure 8.7.

Active Sessions Waiting: Concurrency

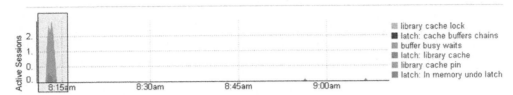

Figure 8.7: *The OEM Display for Active Sessions Waiting on Concurrency*

This display is also a learning aid because OEM lists all of the sources of concurrency waits including library cache lock, latch, and buffer busy waits, and it also displays the values associated with each concurrency component. When the chosen snapshot is double clicked, OEM delivers a summary histogram of the response time components for the top ten SQL statements and top ten sessions that were identified during the AWR snapshot as shown in Figure 8.8.

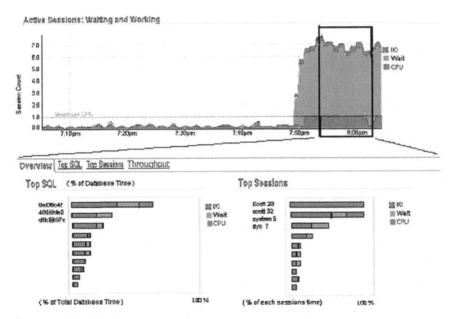

Figure 8.8: *The OEM Top Ten SQL and Top Ten Session Response Time Component Display*

Oracle Troubleshooting

This visual display of summary information allows the quick identification of the most resource-intensive tasks. In addition, it can instantly be seen if the main response time component is I/O, CPU, or Oracle internal wait events. Oracle performance investigations that used to take hours are now completed in a matter of seconds.

While this functionality of OEM is amazing in its own right, Oracle 10g has taken the AWR model beyond the intelligent display of performance metrics. Using true Artificial Intelligence (AI), Oracle Enterprise Manager now has a built-in interface to the Automatic Database Diagnostic Monitor (ADDM), and the intelligent SQL Tuning Advisor.

The main OEM performance screen displays a summary of session wait time server-side components as shown in Figure 8.9. Understanding the components involved in total response time can give huge insight into the root cause of a performance bottleneck.

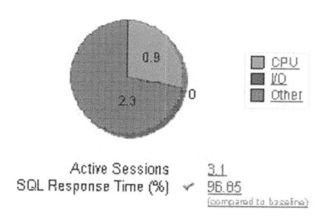

Figure 8.9: *Active Session Response Time OEM Summary Display*

In this figure, there are currently 3.1 active sessions with approximately one-third of the response time being consumed in CPU activities, which is a very common profile for 10g databases with large data caches. The figure also includes the important SQL Response Time (%) delta metric that displays marginal changes on overall SQL performance.

The OEM interface to ASH also allows drilling down and viewing details on any of the active Oracle session. Figure 8.10 shows the hyperlinks to detailed session statistics, wait events, open cursors and locks associated with the task.

Session Details: SID 42

Collected From Target

General | Statistics Wait Events Open Cursors Locks

Serial Number **52801**	Logged On Since	**2003-08-13 08:22:58.0**
Current Status **INACTIVE**	Last Activity On	**2003-08-13 09:09:57.0**
Wait Event **IDLE**	Connection Type	**DEDICATED**
OS Server Process ID **2445**	SQL ID	**No currently executing SQL**
DB User Name **OLAF**		
Resource Consumer Group **0**		

Application Information

Program **JDBC Thin Client**
Module **Oracle Enterprise Manager**
Command **UNKNOWN**

Client Information

OS Client Process ID **1234**
OS User Name **0**
Terminal **0**

Figure 8.10: *Session Level Detail Display in OEM*

Conclusion

This chapter has shown that real-time wait event information is captured in *v$* views and 10046 trace files. For an extra cost, Oracle provides the Active Session History views which relieves the DBA from the tedium of detailed trace setup. The main points of this chapter include:

- ASH is not required: All ASH functionality can be captured with free, traditional techniques.

- ASH captures wait event details: The *v$active_session_history* view collects wait state details every 60 seconds and stores them in a rolling buffer.

- For long-term retention, the data from *v$active_session_history* is transferred to *dba_hist_active_sess_history* whenever one takes an AWR snapshot.

- OEM performance pack and diagnostic pack have a visual interface into the ASH views, but specialized trending tools can also be used to identify trends and signatures in wait events.

Book Conclusion

Oracle troubleshooting has been the focus of this book with hopes of educating the reader in ways to accomplish emergency as well as long-term solutions for database problems. There are many ways to go about solving particular concerns of Oracle users and this book gives insight into several silver bullets, but not nearly encompassing all the different avenues one can take to resolve one's issues. Various ways to investigate problems in the DBA's database, such as ratio-based and bottleneck analysis, were covered in detail.

Next, performance, storage, table and memory issues were addressed with several scripts given to solve various situations. Following that were chapters dedicated to the Oracle System Global Area (SGA), troubleshooting the shared pool, the log buffer, sorting and I/O as well as quite a bit of attention given to solving problems with SQL.

The final chapter concerned using the Automatic Session History (ASH) in Oracle, which is a data collection mechanism that keeps highly detailed session information for a short period of time.

It is the hope of Rampant Books and the authors that this book was helpful in showing the reader many avenues in troubleshooting Oracle databases and making the job just a little bit easier.

Index

About the Authors

Robin Schumacher serves as the Worldwide Director of Product Management for MySQL, the world's leading open-source database management system. Robin has over fourteen years experience in database administration, development, monitoring, and tuning with Oracle, DB2, Teradata, Sybase, and Microsoft SQL Server.

He has authored countless performance-related articles for many database-centric magazines as well as serving as a database software reviewer and feature writer for the likes of Intelligent Enterprise, eWeek, DM Review, and others.

 **Donald K. Burleson** is one of the world's top Oracle Database experts with more than 20 years of full-time DBA experience. He specializes in creating database architectures for very large online databases and he has worked with some of the world's most powerful and complex systems.

A former Adjunct Professor, Don Burleson has written 30 books, published more than 100 articles in National Magazines, and serves as Editor-in-Chief of Rampant TechPress. Don is a popular lecturer and teacher and is a frequent speaker at Oracle Openworld and other international database conferences.

Made in the USA
Columbia, SC
15 May 2022

60340916R00117